The Sower Soweth The Word

The Sower Soweth The Word

"Excerpts From The

Heart Of An Itinerant Preacher"

Gary B. Bailey

Reach The World Publishing

Copyright © 2015 by Gary Bailey

Reach The World Publishing
PO Box 262
Hyde, PA 16843
www.garybaileyministries.com.com

First Printing, May, 2015
Printed in the United States of America

All rights reserved under International Copyright Law. Reproduction of text or cover in whole or in part without the express written consent by the author is not permitted and is unlawful according to the 1976 United States Copyright Act.
"How To Write A Thank you note" by Tim Stemple used by permission
Foreword by Rev. Jay Francis

The Sower Soweth The Word: Excerpts From The Heart Of An Itinerant Preacher
ISBN-13:978-1-943256-00-6
ISBN-10:1943256004

Unless otherwise indicated, all Scripture quotations are taken from the **King James Version** of the Bible.

Scripture quotations marked (**AMP**) are taken from the Amplified Bible, Copyright © 1954, 1958, 1962, 1964, 1965, 1987 by The Lockman Foundation. Used by permission.

Reach The World Publishing

Dedication

This book is dedicated to that great cloud of witnesses: Gospel laborers who have gone before us blazing a trail for those of us who follow after.

Kenneth E. (Dad) Hagin, a Father in the faith to me and the founder of Rhema Bible Training College (my alma mater); A great man of love and faith; Kenneth W. Hagin who has worked tirelessly to establish RBTC as a premier school of Christian ministry here in the U.S. and around the world.

Rev. John Hendricks was the resident theologian and ghost writer for Rex Humbard. John mentored me. He knew the Bible better than anyone I ever met, knew Jesus better than anyone I know and demonstrated a genuine humility in a way I have not seen before or since in anyone.

Rev. Dan Dewitt, befriended and encouraged me as a young minister and Lester Sumrall, my former pastor and mentor.

"Holy" Hubert Lindsay, the purest evangelist I ever met with the greatest passion for lost souls I have ever witnessed.

Among others there were John Osteen; T.L. Osborn; Norvel Hayes; wonderful preachers who fed my spirit and stirred my heart to press further in God.

Then there are the stories of Gospel heroes and champions of the faith. Those who ran the race before me; men and women who faithfully preached the Word and ministered by the Holy Ghost. Peter Cartwright, who toiled relentlessly as a Methodist Circuit rider carrying the Gospel into the untamed wilderness of the United States; George Mueller, a man of great compassion, faith and prayer; Charles Parham and William

Seymour, pioneers of Pentecost; Maria Woodworth Etter; Smith Wigglesworth; F.F. Bosworth; John G. Lake; Aimee Semple McPherson, G.C. Bevington; Alpha Humbard; William Branham; J.R. Goodwin. These are my mentors and my friends and I owe a tremendous debt of gratitude to each one. I could mention many others of whom I have heard preach, read their biographies and followed their example. They have gone before me yet I feel like I know them because of their passion for the things of God.

And to my good friend, Joe Jordan; Joe has the greatest healing ministry along with the most unusual operations of the Holy Spirit that I have ever witnessed. Joe is a true gentleman in the faith, a Bible Scholar, a mentor to me and a close personal friend. We have enjoyed many phone conversations concerning ministry and the things of the Holy Spirit. Joe has encouraged me and proved to be a tremendous example of joy and victory in the Holy Ghost in spite of personal difficulties and setbacks. His steadfastness in adversity and joy in ministry is an inspiration. Joe will be 84 years old this year and He is still going strong in the ministry. This is his 50th year of itinerant ministry. He has had a long run and he will finish strong. Joe Jordan is my good friend and I love him dearly.

Finally, I dedicate this book to the army of young men and women, Gospel Laborers who have heard the call of God and answered. My prayer for them is that they might run their race with courage and joy in the Holy Ghost. I pray that they would have great Christian examples and mentors and that they would be enabled to follow in the steps of holy men and women of God; godly champions of the faith. Let us march on with boldness in our quest for the precious fruit of the earth looking unto Jesus, the Author and Finisher of our faith.

"Oh Lord, give me a backbone as big as a sawlog, ribs like the sleepers under the church floor, put iron shoes on me and galvanized breeches, give me a rhinoceros hide for a skin, and hang a wagonload of determination up in the gable-end of my soul, and help me to sign the contract to fight the devil as long as I've got a fist and bite him as long as I have a tooth, then gum him till I die. All this I ask for Christ's sake. Amen."

Uncle "Bud" Robinson, Nazarene Evangelist (c. 1860-1942)

Contents

Half Title Page
Full Title Page
Information Page
Dedication
Epigraph 1
Contents
Foreword
Preface
Acknowledgment
Introduction
Half Title Page 2
Epigraph 2

Abiding 27
Affecting Heaven 28
Angels 29
Anointing Oil 30
Are Heathen People Really Lost? 32
Ask 33
Back To The Basics 34
Be A Holy Ghost Church 34
Believe The Gospel 36
Blessed To Be A Blessing 36
Book Full Of Promises, A 37
By The Law Is The Knowledge Of Sin 38
Can I Repay Him? 39
Caring One For Another 40
Carrying Forth His Word And Spirit 40
City On A Hill, A 41
Comfortable Living With All Parts 42
Communicate 43
Conquerors Follow Their Dreams 44
Dependent 44

Develop Your Spiritual Senses	45
Developing God's Garden	47
Divine Flow	48
Do Faithfully What You Do	48
Doing The One Thing	50
Don't Be Discouraged	51
Door To The Sheep	51
Elite Disciples	53
Everybody Needs A Preacher	54
Faith And Hope	55
Faith Is An Act	56
Faith Is Released	57
Faith Takes A Nap	58
Faithfulness Cannot Be Separated From Faith	58
Fight On!	59
For Saints And Sinners	60
Fresh Outpouring, A	61
Frustrating The Devil's Plan	62
Fulfilling Desires	63
Genuine Gospel, The	63
Genuine Success	64
Gift Given, A Gift Received, A	65
Give The Devil A Fit	66
Give Yourself Away	69
Giving Expresses God's Love	70
Goal, The	71
God Himself	72
God Is Not Finished With Us	72
God Is Our Source Of Supply	73
God Is Working In You	74
God Speaks	75
God With Us	77
Good Fight, The	78
Gospel You Hear, The	79
Grace Called Giving, A	80

Grace Is Given To Everyone	81
Grace Of A Willing Heart, The	81
Grace To Serve	82
Greatest Life Changing Force, The	83
Greatest Success In Life, The	83
Greatest Thing In The World, The	85
He Confirms His Word	86
Helped To Help	86
Hidden Treasure	87
Highest And Best, The	88
His Eye Affects His Heart	89
His Hands Were Heavy	91
His Unspeakable Gift	92
Holy Ghost Dependence	92
Holy Ghost Manifestation	93
Honoring God	94
How Many Oak Trees in One Acorn?	95
How Shall They Preach?	96
How To Accomplish Anything	97
I Am A Debtor	98
I Am Not Ashamed	99
I Am Reminded	100
I Cannot Help But Give Again	101
I Cannot Out Give God	102
I Continue To Preach	102
I Desire Fruit	103
I Give Myself To Prayer	103
Identified With Christ	104
Impacting This World And The Next	105
In Everything Give Thanks	106
Included In The Work	107
Jesus Christ Is The Answer	107
Job To Finish And A Work To Be Done, A	108
Just Traveling Through	108
Keep The Floodgates Open	111

Key To A Victorious Ministry, The	112
Knit Together	113
Knowing And Standing In The Will Of God	116
Laborers Together	116
Least Of These, The	118
Liquid Properties Of The Word	118
Living Life From The Inside Out	119
Look For Reward	119
Look On the Fields Of Harvest	120
Look, Pray And Go	121
Lord Is Good To All, The	121
Love Is Greater Than All	122
Lowering And Lifting	124
Make Hay While The Sun Shines!	125
Making A Difference	126
Many Members- One Body	127
Many Small Sacrifices From One Great Sacrifice	127
Meat And Potatoes	129
Mighty Word Of God, The	129
Minister To Your Own Soul	130
Ministry Of Giving	132
Ministry Of Reconciliation	134
Moral Law Of God	135
More Important Than Money	136
Most Effective And Efficient Activity, The	138
Multifaceted Gospel	139
My Friend	140
My Gospel	141
My King	142
Necessary Ingredient, A	142
Necessity Of Gospel Senders	143
New Day With The Promise Of God, A	143
Night And Day Praying	144
No Greater Love	145
No More Bad Days	145

No One Is Exempt	146
No Small Decision	147
On Schedule	149
One Life To Give	149
One Person	150
Open Doors And Open Arms	151
Others	151
Our Battle	152
Our Father's Business	152
Our Joy And Reward	153
Our Own Company	153
Our Wealthy Place	155
Outward Thinkers	156
Part Of Everything We Do, A	157
Payday Is Coming	158
Plan to Go, Plan To Give	159
Pleasing God	159
Pray For Me	160
Prayer And Preaching	160
Praying Out The Will Of God	161
Praying Specifically	162
Praying With All Prayer	163
Preach With Power	163
Prophecy, Dreams And Visions	166
Reaching Beyond	168
Reason We Give, The	169
Reciprocal Action Of God, The	169
Redeemed From The Curse	169
Redeeming The Time	170
Returning Thanks	171
Rewarder, The	172
Run Your Course With Joy	173
Sacrifice Pleasing To God, A	174
Satan is a Defeated Foe!	175
Sealed With The Knowledge Of His Coming	176

Seed Is The Word, The	177
Seed Sowers	178
Seedtime And Harvest	179
Shout Grace!	180
Simple Faith In A Simple Message	181
Simple Plan Of Preaching	181
Smack Dab In The Middle Of God's Perfect Will	182
Sowing God's Word Into Your Heart	183
Speak Good Things	186
Special Providence For The Righteous	186
Spiritual Fathers	188
Spiritual Practice	189
Stewardship Principle	190
Striving Together In Prayer	191
Strong Churches	192
Supply Is In His Name	193
Take Time To Give Thanks	193
Take Time To Pray	193
Tangible And Intangible Fruit	195
Tangible Presence	195
Teach Us To Number Our Days	196
Thanksgiving	197
They Loved Not Their Lives	198
They Will Be Saved	200
This Gospel Shall Be Preached	200
Thrilled With This Gospel	201
Together We Go	202
Together We Win!	203
Tossing Tracts	204
Two Way Street, The	205
Ultimate Gift, The	205
Variety Of Ministry	206
Very Present Help, A	206
We Are Not Saved	207
We Are One Another	207

We Are The Body Of Christ 208
We Have The Message 208
We Must Continue To Preach 209
We Need Each Other 211
We Preach Not Ourselves... 212
Weeping First 212
What Brings Revival? 213
What Is God Doing? 214
Whatsoever Thy Hand Findeth To Do, Do It 215
When A Baby Is Born 216
When We Act In Faith 218
Why Go To All The Trouble?.. 219
Why Of Prosperity.. 219
Wise Thing To Do, A 221
With Help We Go 221
Wonderful Idea, A.. 221
Word Brings Fruit, The 222
Word Is Working, The...223
Word Of God Will Have Its Effect!, The 223
Word We Preach, The 224
Working Together 225
You Are God's Garden..225
You Are The Disciple That Jesus Loves!...................................... 227
You Get What You Preach.. 227

*Appendix: How To Write A Thank You Note 229
Contact The Author..230

Foreword

"For to me to live is Christ, and to die is gain." Philippians 1:21 Spiritual life is maintained and supported by feeding on Him, the Bread of Life. Jesus Christ and His Kingdom dominate the life of this author whose life is spent for the glory of Christ, the good of the church and the spread of the Gospel.

These notes were birthed in a devotional heart pursuing intimacy with the Savior. Carefully read, one's heart will be opened to a deeper Christian life so needed for these perilous times. They are heavenly food for the soul!

My growing friendship with Pastor Gary is inspiring due to his passionate love and allegiance to Christ which neither life nor death can destroy. I know his passion is for bringing believers to their highest potential in Christ.

This excellent collection is a reminder to keep our eyes focused on Christ as we pray and believe for a Great Awakening. It contains excellent exhortations to sustain one's faith and teaching that will mature the Believer and kindle a strong hope for the future. I highly recommend this book, <u>The Sower Soweth the Word</u>, as a daily resource for your devotional time.

Because of Calvary,
Rev. Jay T. Francis
Director IAM Ministers' Fellowship
Pastor Rock Road Chapel Ministries

A Prayer of David

Cause me to hear thy lovingkindness in the morning; for in thee do I trust: cause me to know the way wherein I should walk; for I lift up my soul unto thee. Deliver me, O Lord, from mine enemies: I flee unto thee to hide me. Teach me to do thy will; for thou art my God: thy spirit is good; lead me into the land of uprightness. Quicken me, O Lord, for thy name's sake: for thy righteousness 'sake bring my soul out of trouble. And of thy mercy cut off mine enemies, and destroy all them that afflict my soul: for I am thy servant.
Psalm 143:8-12

Preface

It has been my privilege to declare this Glorious Gospel Message for nearly forty years. I have been granted the opportunity to preach and teach by churches, pastors, ministers and missionaries. For these I am grateful. For more than twenty years it has been my habit to sit down each month and write a thank you note to those who helped me get to where I am going and get me back home again. Each thank you note I write includes a short meditation or teaching. This book is a result of those notes that I have compiled through the years. As you will see, there is a recurring theme running through the book addressing ministry, prayer, the necessity of preaching, stewardship and thankfulness. My hope is that you will find something within these pages that will inspire, strengthen and encourage you in your daily walk with God.

The Author
March 17, 2015
Curwensville, Pennsylvania

Acknowledgment

Thanks to those who by their faithful support and prayers have sent me to preach this Glorious Gospel. By their help I continue to be inspired and refreshed in my pursuit of the Kingdom of God and His call upon my life.

My sincere thanks to the many pastors who have opened their churches and pulpits to me. I have a great respect for these godly leaders. I am a friend to pastors. I appreciate pastors.

Special thanks to Tim Stemple who, in spite of all the books that have been written, gave me a reason to write my own book and taught me how to write a thank you note. *(See appendix p.229)

Thanks to my parents, who raised me in church and encouraged me to do the right thing. Thanks to my first church family who instilled in me a love for God and the saints. Dad was my best supporter until his passing in 2011. I was adopted as an infant and my Mother's prayer (like that of Hannah's in the Bible) was; "God, if you will give him to me to raise, I will give him back to you when he is old enough." At eighteen years of age I left home and headed off to Bible School.

Thanks to my daughters, Rebekah, Kari, Anna and Sarah. You have brought an abundance of beauty, love, wit and laughter into our household. I am extremely proud of each one of you. Lastly, Thanks to my wife. Gwen, you have patiently stood by me, loved me, prayed for me, and believed in me. You have been good company through our many years together. You are my best friend, my sweetheart, my prayer partner, the mother of our children and my sister in Christ. You are a woman of strong faith and character whom I greatly admire. I am pleased to share my life with you and be called your husband.

Introduction

This book is the result of years spent in itinerant ministry. Each month I sit down to share my thoughts and thank those who sent me on the wings of their prayers and financial support. I put together these writings with the intention of sharing some of the ponderings and meditations of my heart.

Within these pages are golden nuggets of truth that will bless you. The readings are gleaned from twenty years of scripture meditations included in my thank you notes to partners of our ministry. The contents are arranged in alphabetical order by subheadings so that you can quickly turn to a particular segment of the book.

My intention is to give you spiritual nuggets for meditation and reflection. I suppose it is more of a devotional than anything else. The subject matter varies but usually returns to ministry and the commission of Christ to go preach.

As you read these pages your heart will be stirred anew for the Church and the work of God in the earth. The mindset is that of a traveling preacher and teacher. There is a spark of the evangelist's fire and the itinerant ministry is highlighted. Jesus was an itinerant evangelist. Luke 4:43-44 reveals His passion to go and preach. *And he said unto them, I must preach the kingdom of God to other cities also: for therefore am I sent. 44 And he preached in the synagogues of Galilee.*

I love the Church of God in all its divergent glory. As you read, I trust that you will be stirred in your heart to satisfy the call of God on your life whatever that might be. My prayer is that you develop a renewed passion for reaching a lost world and a revived love for the Church of our Lord Jesus Christ.

The Sower Soweth
The Word

I cried, "Lord I will go.
Where shall I go?"
And Jesus said,
"Go here, go there,
wherever souls are perishing."
M.B.W. Etter (c. 1844-1924)

Abiding

We can have fruit because we are linked together with others and the entire Body of Christ. Jesus said in John's Gospel: I am the vine, ye are the branches: He that abideth in me, and I in him, the same bringeth forth much fruit: for without me ye can do nothing. (John 15:5). When we stay connected with Jesus we bear fruit. If we are not connected, we cannot bear fruit. It is silly to think that a peach branch separated from a peach tree could continue to grow and develop fruit on its own. It is just as absurd to think that we can bring forth fruit separated from Jesus. The scriptures say that we are to abide in Him. Abiding is not automatic. It involves a conscious choice. We must abide on purpose. Abide with intent. Again, Jesus said: And he said to them all, If any man will come after me, let him deny himself, and take up his cross daily, and follow me. (Luke 9:23). There is a sacrifice involved in abiding. As we see from the above verse, to come after or follow Jesus we must 1) deny ourselves and 2) take up our cross. Abiding in Christ means 1) not abiding in our own pleasure, will or concern. And 2) it means giving ourselves to His pleasure, will and concern. Our abiding is to be daily and consistent. Abiding is another word for fellowship. We are to fellowship in His Word, fellowship in prayer and fellowship in His will along with others. In our abiding we feel what He feels, see what He sees and know what He knows. We speak much of the fact that Jesus is touched with the feeling of our infirmities. (Hebrews 4:15). This is true but in our abiding we experience His heart. We feel what He feels and His concern is our concern. We enjoy His mighty deeds but more importantly in our abiding we understand His ways. We see this distinction between the children of Israel and Moses: He made known his ways unto Moses, his acts unto the children of Israel. (Psalm 103:7) Our heart begins to beat with His Great Heart. Abide in Him. This is where the true riches are. This is where the exhilaration and satisfaction of our life in Him is at its pinnacle. Above all else, the one thing the Holy Spirit is impressing upon Believers' hearts and minds is to abide in Him. And now, little children, abide in him; that, when he shall appear, we may have confidence, and not be ashamed before him at his coming. (1 John 2:28).

Affecting Heaven

Paul understood that even though he was the recipient of their gift it was also a sacrifice offered up to God, received by God in Heaven. When sacrifices go up blessing comes down. That is why Paul could say to the Philippians with confidence in verse 19, "But my God shall supply all your need according to his riches in glory by Christ Jesus." As offerings go up good gifts come down. When we give as unto the Lord, there He receives our offering and we in turn can expect benefits to be poured on us from heaven. The scriptures speak of a variety of spiritual sacrifices we can offer up to God. "Ye also, as lively stones, are built up a spiritual house, an holy priesthood, to offer up spiritual sacrifices, acceptable to God by Jesus Christ." (1 Peter 2:5). The Word of God speaks of praise, thanksgiving, tithes, offerings, doing good, prayers, almsgivings and even our faith are spiritual sacrifices offered up to God. You can be sure that as prayers go up, blessing comes down, as praises go up benefits come down, as tithes and offerings go up, the supply of His Spirit comes down. There is a relationship between heaven and earth. Our actions on earth will affect what goes on in heaven. Your offerings move heaven. James tells us, "Every good gift and every perfect gift is from above, and cometh down from the Father of lights, with whom is no variableness, neither shadow of turning." (James 1:17).

Angels

God is not unrighteous to forget your work and labour of love, which ye have shewed toward his name, in that ye have ministered to the saints, and do minister. (Hebrews 6:10) It seems that according to the Word of God that angels are aware of good deeds done and are actively observing our actions. What is the reason? I am sure there is some record keeping and most likely some curiosity concerning all things mortal. At any rate, I believe angels are busy around the clock. There are scriptures that give us some idea that Angels are aware of our actions. What we do for others does not go unnoticed in the realm of the spirit. Angels appeared in human form and our activities provide entertainment for angels! Let brotherly love continue. Be not forgetful to entertain strangers: for thereby some have entertained angels unawares. (Hebrews 13:1-2). ...which things the angels desire to look into. (1 Peter 1:12). ...for we are made a spectacle unto the world, and to angels, and to men. (1 Corinthians 4:9). ... seen of angels, (1 Tim 3:16). Angels are given charge to protect us and watch over our lives. Everyone on earth has been assigned an angel. Whether born again or not, angels are protecting and watching over people. We who are in the know can take advantage and put our angels to work for us. By acknowledging Christ and speaking the Word of God, angels will minister for us according to the will of God. By giving and doing for others you permit angels to minister on your behalf. Bless the LORD, ye his angels, that excel in strength, that do his commandments, hearkening unto the voice of his word. (Psalm 103:20). But to which of the angels said he at any time, Sit on my right hand, until I make thine enemies thy footstool? Are they not all ministering spirits, sent forth to minister for them who shall be heirs of salvation? (Hebrews 1:13-14). Your angel is watching you!

Anointing Oil

Behold, how good and how pleasant it is for brethren to dwell together in unity! 2 It is like the precious ointment upon the head, that ran down upon the beard, even Aaron's beard: that went down to the skirts of his garments; 3 As the dew of Hermon, and as the dew that descended upon the mountains of Zion: for there the Lord commanded the blessing, even life for evermore. (Psalm 133). We need each other. I am a lifeline to others and others provide a lifeline for me. If it is a two-man job I cannot do it by myself. God commands His blessing when we work and flow together. It is the anointing that brings us together. It is the anointing that breaks every yoke of bondage and sets the captive free. Just as the above scripture illustrates, the anointing flows down from the head and touches the whole body. There is a quality in oil that gets on everything. When oil is introduced it flows into the smallest nook and lubricates every little thing.

Because of this tendency, oil is used in engineering to keep everything running smoothly. Vehicles, machinery and anything that moves and interacts with other moving parts needs oil or some form of lubrication. This is the purpose of God's anointing oil. The anointing brings us together and helps us work and flow together. One is anointed for one purpose and another for another purpose but it is the oil of anointing that gets the job done. Without it, everything grinds to a screeching halt. Just as any piece of machinery with moving parts needs lubrication, so does the Body of Christ. Communication is the grease that makes everything work. When we "communicate" with God through His Word and prayer, obeying His command, we receive anointing oil to function in our calling. When we "communicate" with one another that anointing oil is passed on and lubricates the whole body. When we pray for others, when we give to others and when we make an effort to interact with others in the Body of Christ the anointing oil flows. When this anointing oil is flowing God commands blessing. When we flow together and work together God commands blessing. When we cooperate and communicate, God commands blessing. This communication creates a flow of anointing that keeps everything running smoothly and God's blessing is abundant. I communicate with others and they communicate with me. God is the one who anoints us and equips us and blesses us. God gives us lubricating oil so that we can flow together and work together. What we do we do not do alone. The anointing of God brings us together and we are able to flow and move together in the power and ability of God. This is the anointing. We are anointed together.

Are Heathen People Really Lost?

I went to India for the first time in 1981. India is a beautiful nation filled with beautiful people. At the time of my visit there were seven hundred million people in India. Today, as of this writing, there are one billion two hundred million people in India. I have made five trips and I continue to go. India's population growth has outpaced the evangelistic efforts put forth. Forty two percent of India is still considered unreached. So what about those who have never heard? Are they lost forever? Will God judge them for not believing on Jesus Christ? God is just and they will not be guilty of not believing on Jesus nevertheless they are still guilty and will be condemned. Why? Because the Bible is plain to say that there is none righteous not even one and all have sinned and come short of the glory of God. (See Romans 3:10 and 3:23). The heathen may not be guilty of not believing on Jesus but they are guilty. They are guilty first because God's law was written in their hearts and they are without excuse. They know right from wrong. They are guilty, second because what can be known of God has been revealed in creation. They knew God but did not glorify Him as God. The Gospel is written in the sky and on the sea. The stars of heaven reveal the Creator. In this condition men and women face a dilemma. They know there is a God because of creation and they know that they are responsible for their actions because the law of God is written in their hearts. The heathen have ignored the Truth they have known and their hearts are darkened. At one time they recognized God but did not glorify and acknowledge him as God so they were shut out. The Bible says there foolish hearts were darkened. What of those who acknowledge God without hearing the Gospel? What about those who endeavor to satisfy the requirements of the law written in their hearts? God will move heaven and earth to get the message to them so that they might be saved. The truth is in this condition; if men do not gain knowledge of the truth they could go either way. Some may yield to God but they still must know to whom they must surrender. Some may harden their hearts and only by hearing the Gospel can they be turned. For those who seek God with all their hearts, He will be found of them. There are countless stories of heathen people finding God having been isolated from any Gospel message or Gospel workers. Because they sought the true and living God, God somehow delivered the Gospel to them. Jeremiah said this, "Then shall ye call upon me, and ye shall go and pray unto me, and I will hearken unto you. 13 And ye shall seek me, and find me, when ye shall search for me with all your heart. "(Jeremiah 29:12-13). If this is the case, why not wait until the heathen call on God? They may never do it. This is why we need to preach. Preaching creates an impetus in men's hearts to call upon God. It is by the foolishness of preaching that men are saved. Those who are seeking God when they hear the Gospel will turn to God and be saved. Those who are not seeking will be stirred in their hearts to receive Christ. This Gospel must be preached. We must take it to the ends of the earth. When men and women hear they can be saved. A preacher must be sent to them. Let's take this Gospel to hurting humanity.

Ask

Ask of me, and I shall give thee the heathen for thine inheritance, and the uttermost parts of the earth for thy possession. (Psalm 2:8). The first and most important aspect of being a soul-winner is a desire to see souls saved. Ask God.

Back To The Basics

For by grace are ye saved through faith; and that not of yourselves: it is the gift of God: (Ephesians 2:8). Our faith is the most precious gift that we have from God. I read where a celebrity said once that he envied those who had faith in God. When one realizes that all men do not have faith it makes it all the more precious. If there is one thing the devil is after it is our faith. That is why we must fight the good fight of faith (1 Timothy 6:12). Jesus prayed for Peter that his faith would not fail. And the Lord said, Simon, Simon, behold, Satan hath desired to have you, that he may sift you as wheat: 32 But I have prayed for thee, that thy faith fail not: and when thou art converted, strengthen thy brethren. (Luke 22:31-32). When I struggle with faith issues, I go back to the basics. I played sports in high school and one thing the coaches emphasized over and over was fundamentals. In football it was run, block, tackle, keep your head low and don't hold the ball like a loaf of bread. We practiced the basics over and over until they were second nature. So it is with faith in God. Go back over the basics. Return to your first love. Be sure you are listening to those who are promoting and teaching Bible faith and not the latest preaching fad. Receive God's Word as it is in Truth- THE WORD OF GOD! Believe it just like it is written. The Bible is God's love letter to us and faith will come and faith will grow by the Word of God. Hear it and receive it. Apply it to your life. Your faith will keep you and you will keep your faith strong. Do not doubt with doubters. Get with Believers and believe with Believers.

Be A Holy Ghost Church

God means for His Church to be filled with the Holy Ghost. I mean for churches to be Holy Ghost Churches. Meaning? I mean be filled with the Holy Spirit and stay filled with the Holy Spirit. I mean don't be drunk with wine but be filled with the Spirit. I mean enjoy your own personal Pentecost. I mean have a book of Acts experience! Be filled with the Holy Ghost with the evidence of speaking in other tongues. The new wine is better! Just like the apostles of old, Jesus' Brethren and Mary, the Mother of Jesus. These along with others were in the upper room when the Holy Spirit was initially poured out on the day of Pentecost. Receive this Biblical and scriptural work of grace in your life and in your church. Before Dad Hagin went home to be with the Lord in 2003 he encouraged pastors and churches not only to be Word Churches but also to be Holy Ghost Churches. Specifically, he mentioned in prophecy, "Make your Church not only a Word Church but a Holy Ghost Church." Through the years wherever the church has ears to hear, I have been preaching, "Make Your Church a Holy Ghost Church!" Paul speaks about the operation of the Holy Spirit in the local church in 1 Corinthians chapter fourteen. He speaks of the operation of spiritual gifts and their proper use and order. When things are done decently and in order God can move in an unprecedented fashion. The greatest moves of the Spirit will take place where there is an attention to order. Churches that move in the good order laid out in chapter fourteen of 1 Corinthians, will experience the greatest move of the Spirit in their midst. I have been involved in Spirit filled churches for over three decades and God intends for the move of the Spirit to function in the local church. There is something missing in a church that does not have the move of the Spirit. Many have wondered what is the missing ingredient but could not put their finger on it. The thing that is missing is the manifestation of the Spirit in the local church with an understanding of how to operate the gifts decently and in order. Tongues, interpretation of tongues and prophecy; these along with the other gifts belong in the church of the Lord Jesus.

Believe The Gospel

Thank God for the Gospel! It is a saving Word; it is a healing Word; it is a Word that sets the captives free. We are delivering living bread, bringing refreshment and revival wherever we go. This Gospel is the power of God. Paul was not ashamed of the Gospel because he saw lives transformed and changed. I am not ashamed of this Gospel because I see lives transformed and changed. When people believe the message they are saved, healed, delivered and transformed in every area of life. Bodies are healed, marriages are saved and hurting people are made whole by the preaching of His Word and the operation of the Spirit of God. This is a world shaking, life-changing message. When you believe this Word you are changed by it. The key is to believe. Believe and you can receive it! Receive the promises! Receive the blessings! Become a partaker of the divine nature. How we approach the Word of this Gospel makes all the difference. The Apostle Paul noted that when men believe and receive the Word as it is in truth, the Word of God works powerfully. For this cause also thank we God without ceasing, because, when ye received the word of God which ye heard of us, ye received it not as the word of men, but as it is in truth, the word of God, which effectually worketh also in you that believe. (1 Thessalonians 2:13). Believe the Gospel! It will transform you and make you!

Blessed To Be A Blessing

And all these blessings shall come on thee, and overtake thee, if thou shalt hearken unto the voice of the LORD thy God. Blessed shalt thou be in the city, and blessed shalt thou be in the field. (Deuteronomy 28:2-3). We are blessed to be a blessing. It is important that we stay filled up so we can continue to pour ourselves out in ministry to others.

A Book Full Of Promises

We are taking the Word of God to those who are thirsty. This is our Kingdom venture. It is good news that we are preaching. God is a good God and He has good things for us! When the Word is received and believed, a person cannot help but smile. Why? There is a book full of promises for you and me! Some never get past the thought that this is too good to be true and they walk away never to realize the blessed promises of God. They continue to struggle hoping for something better, wishing their life was different. Not so for us who are in the Kingdom of God. We have access to all of God and all that God has. God Himself is our exceeding great reward and all that He is and has belongs to us! Look at the following two scriptures: After these things the word of the LORD came unto Abram in a vision, saying, Fear not, Abram: I am thy shield, and thy exceeding great reward. (Genesis 15:1). He that spared not his own Son, but delivered him up for us all, how shall he not with him also freely give us all things? (Romans 8:32). Now, if that is just a fairy tale, I am not moved. But this is the Word of God! This is Truth! Now expressions from scripture like "joy unspeakable and full of glory", "peace that passes all understanding", "In thy presence is fullness of joy" and on and on and so on and so forth.... These precious promises all begin to make sense for those who know their God. The Kingdom does not consist of meat and drink but righteousness, peace and joy in the Holy Ghost! It is no wonder Job said: At destruction and famine thou shalt laugh... (Job 5:22). One of the greatest manifestations of faith is joy and laughter. You will laugh when you believe the promises of God! At the very least they will put a smile on your face!

By The Law Is The Knowledge Of Sin

Occasionally I have preached in the open air on college campuses. The young people we preach to have little to no knowledge of the Truth. These are not those who have come to a church service or revival meeting knowing they are going to hear the Gospel. These are those who are atheistic, agnostic and indifferent to God and eternity. They are unaware of their lost condition. Our goal is to plant the seed of the Word in their lives. I have preached to and confronted Muslims, Jewish Professors and even Christians who were unsure of their faith. Some were antagonistic and hostile. Others listened intently. My heart breaks for these young people. So confused by conflicting ideas and philosophies. Some are genuinely seeking for Truth, others are there to party and have a good time. They have need of a Savior but do not realize their own need. They have a problem but they do not know what their problem is. Matthew 1:21 reveals the problem and the answer. "And she shall bring forth a son, and thou shalt call his name JESUS: for he shall save his people from their sins." The problem is sin and the answer is Jesus Christ. The need is to convince sinners they have a sin problem and are in need of a Savior. The law of God is the means whereby sinners may be convinced and convicted of sin. The law reveals the problem. The Law (the bad news), must be preached before the Gospel (the good news), can be received. Sinners must be convicted before they are converted. When the law is presented skillfully, the hearts of sinners are properly prepared to receive the Gospel. Christians also need to hear the law of God because the law identifies sin. Christians must have knowledge of the law in order to deal with sin in their own lives. The Law of God causes us to recognize sin in our lives and make us aware of God's standard of holiness and right living. Now, through the preaching of the Gospel, we can receive grace and ability from God to live, as we ought. "Now we know that what things soever the law saith, it saith to them who are under the law: that every mouth may be stopped, and all the world may become guilty before God. Therefore by the deeds of the law there shall no flesh be justified in his sight: for by the law is the knowledge of sin." (Romans 3:19-20).

Can I Repay Him?

Can we repay God for what He has done? Never. We can however, acknowledge His goodness by being thankful. I owe Him everything. I cannot repay Him and any attempt to do so would be an embarrassment. I can give Him my life. I can be a thankful person. The most we can do is acknowledge the debt we owe. To be genuinely thankful comes nearest to repaying Him. I am truly thankful to God for the things He has done for me. I owe Him everything but I can only give Him my thanks. I want to live my life in a way that will show God and people that I am grateful for all that I am and have. Genuine thankfulness and humility are intertwined. Humility is the ability to receive from God and others. Humility will take you further in life than any other character trait. God can bless humble and grateful people. He blesses the thankful. When things around us are bad, God is always good. Because we belong to Him, we partake of His goodness. God is for us, He is with us and He is in us. As we acknowledge Him through our thankfulness, He shows Himself strong on our behalf. I thank God for the people in my life. They are God's blessing to me. Thankfulness toward God and people is a reflection of the character of God in our lives. People are a reminder of God's goodness in my life and I am grateful. Be blessed and find someone and say thank you. God's smile is on the life of the thankful.

Caring One For Another

That there should be no schism in the body; but that the members should have the same care one for another. 26 And whether one member suffer, all the members suffer with it; or one member be honoured, all the members rejoice with it. 27 Now ye are the body of Christ, and members in particular. (1 Corinthians 12:25-27). Gifts and help from the Body of Christ is evidence to hurting people that they are not without God or hope in this world. When those who freely give meet our needs, it provides reassurance that God loves us and that He is aware of our circumstances. It also enables us to freely give to others. 8 And God is able to make all grace abound toward you; that ye, always having all sufficiency in all things, may abound to every good work: 9 (As it is written, He hath dispersed abroad; he hath given to the poor: his righteousness remaineth for ever. (2 Corinthians 9:8-9).

Carrying Forth His Word And Spirit

My job as a minister of the Gospel is to impart the Word and Spirit wherever I go. I am a preacher so through that avenue I am able to impart the Word and the Spirit. My mission statement could be summed up from this mighty scripture in Luke's Gospel: The Spirit of the Lord is upon me, because he hath anointed me to preach the gospel to the poor; he hath sent me to heal the brokenhearted, to preach deliverance to the captives, and recovering of sight to the blind, to set at liberty them that are bruised, To preach the acceptable year of the Lord. (Luke 4:18-19). This, of course, was the mission statement for Christ's earthly ministry. After

His unique work of atonement through His death, burial and resurrection, after rising from the dead Jesus later appeared and said to His disciples and to all who will follow him closely: Peace be unto you: as my Father hath sent me, even so send I you. (John 20:20-21). "As my Father hath sent me, even so send I you." We are sent ones anointed by God to carry forth His Word and Spirit. Another venue we have to minister the Word and Spirit is through the avenue of song. In the New Testament songs are meant to minister the Word: Let the word of Christ dwell in you richly in all wisdom; teaching and admonishing one another in psalms and hymns and spiritual songs, singing with grace in your hearts to the Lord. (Colossians 3:16). And the Spirit: And be not drunk with wine, wherein is excess; but be filled with the Spirit; 19 Speaking to yourselves in psalms and hymns and spiritual songs, singing and making melody in your heart to the Lord; (Ephesians 5:18-19). The door is open. Through preaching, teaching and song let us take the Word and the Spirit to a world that desperately needs it.

A City On A Hill

We have a treasure and it will not be hidden! Jesus said; Ye are the light of the world. A city that is set on an hill cannot be hid. 15 Neither do men light a candle, and put it under a bushel, but on a candlestick; and it giveth light unto all that are in the house. 16 Let your light so shine before men, that they may see your good works, and glorify your Father which is in heaven. (Matthew 5:14-16). We have endeavored to preach wherever and whenever doors opened to us. We have crisscrossed this nation with the Gospel. We are reaching out to the nations of the world. We minister to a multitude of people giving them the Word and the Spirit. Jesus is lifted up wherever we go. We minister the uncompromised Word Of

God in person and distribute gospel seeds: any media available to us. These efforts see people saved, healed and filled with the Spirit of God. The Word goes forth in freedom and power. The Gospel we preach has impacted many lives as we take this Good News to anyone who has ears to hear. What about the future? Jesus is coming soon. The world grows darker but our light is shining brighter and our Blessed Hope grows stronger! This Gospel must be preached in all the world for a witness. We continue to take this Gospel to the world! We will shout it from the housetops. Our city is set on a hill!

Comfortable Living With All Parts

The Church of The Lord Jesus Christ is vast and varied. The Body of Christ is multifaceted. O, how we need a revelation of the benefit of different! The Church is strong because we are made up of many parts and whether or not we realize it we need every single part! We do not and cannot function independently of one another. As I travel from place to place and experience various aspects of the Church, the Body of Christ, I am convinced more than ever that we all need each other. Even though at times I deal with those who seemingly need nothing, in truth, they are more needy than most. One may not be immediately aware of their need for others as Paul mentioned in 1 Corinthians chapter twelve: And the eye cannot say unto the hand, I have no need of thee: nor again the head to the feet, I have no need of you. 22 Nay, much more those members of the body, which seem to be more feeble, are necessary: (1Corinthians 12:21-22). In the natural, the smallest member of our bodies is necessary. The little toe, the little finger or a toenail! Having all my body parts makes for comfortable living and anyone who has lost even the smallest body member knows what I am talking about. Paul, in chapter twelve is speaking of the Body of

Christ and ministry gifts. This passage can be applied to an individual Body of Believers but I believe Paul is dealing with much more than the local church. He is talking about the local church receiving ministry gifts that are different. As valuable and precious as our own gifts are, they cannot fully supply every need. Other "differing" gifts are available to meet those needs if we will receive them. No one can take the pastors place. Paul says there are only SOME pastors and only SOME apostles and SOME evangelists and SOME prophets and teachers. And God hath set some in the church, first apostles, secondarily prophets, thirdly teachers, after that miracles, then gifts of healings, helps, governments, diversities of tongues. (1 Corinthians 12:28). As precious and valuable as any one gifting is, one can only present the gift and anointing that he has. God has given DIFFERENT gifts and in order to grow up in him, we need all of them.

Communicate

In the book of Galatians Paul talks about communicating with those who minister the Word of God. "Let him that is taught in the word communicate unto him that teacheth in all good things." (Galatians 6:6). Notice that it says let him that is taught communicate or give to him that teaches. When we are taught the Word of God, according to scripture we are to give to the ones who teach us. In this way we will sow good things and reap good things. If we do not give when we are taught the Word of God we are still sowing and we will still reap but now we are sowing to the flesh. In other words when we are in the habit of hearing the Word of God and giving to the man of God or woman of God who preaches and teaches, we are sowing good seed and we will reap the appropriate harvest. If we are hearing the Word without giving we are still sowing and we will reap accordingly. If we read on in

Galatians you will see what I mean. "Be not deceived; God is not mocked: for whatsoever a man soweth, that shall he also reap. For he that soweth to his flesh shall of the flesh reap corruption; but he that soweth to the Spirit shall of the Spirit reap life everlasting." (Galatians 6:7-8). When we give or when we do not give we are still sowing seed. When we have heard the Word of God taught and give we are sowing to the Spirit. When we have heard the Word of God taught and do not give we are sowing to the flesh. So where does our responsibility lie? Whenever the Word of God is ministered to us we ought to give, as we are able. This is sowing to the Spirit. God's Word will continue to go forth and we will be blessed.

Conquerors Follow Their Dreams

It is my dream to touch the nations of the earth with the Gospel of Christ. I know that this is not a task for one person alone. Others must dream a similar dream. Will you dream with me? I know that God has given you a dream and it is my desire to see your dreams fulfilled. When we delight in Him, He will give us the desires of our heart. So many times I have been tempted to get discouraged, to quit in midstream but I know there is no quitting for Conquerors and we are more than Conquerors! I am motivated to higher heights, to labor more for the Master, to accomplish more for the Kingdom of God. I rejoice to know there are others willing to sacrifice and give for the furtherance of the Gospel of Christ. Your dream will come true. Christ has made us more than conquerors and conquerors follow their dreams!

Dependent

We are enabled and strengthened by the prayers of others. We are blessed and helped by those who give in support of our ministry. The business of giving and receiving is interwoven into the fabric of the body of Christ. What we do, we do not do alone. We are dependent upon each other in the Body of Christ and giving and receiving clearly shows this. I know that many would like to be independently wealthy; exempt from receiving from others when it comes to finance but the truth is, God set it up so that we must depend upon each other. I am not complete without you and you are not complete without me. We need each other! Paul makes this very point in his letter to the Philippians. 2 Grace be unto you, and peace, from God our Father, and from the Lord Jesus Christ. 3 I thank my God upon every remembrance of you, 4 Always in every prayer of mine for you all making request with joy, 5 For your fellowship in the gospel from the first day until now; 6 Being confident of this very thing, that he which hath begun a good work in you will perform it until the day of Jesus Christ: (Philippians 1:2-6). Paul is saying that the work God is doing in their lives is directly related to their fellowship (i.e. communication, distribution and contribution), in the Gospel of Christ. Together we complete each other! The tendency of some is to go it alone but God says different. Our dependence is to be on Him and upon one another in the Body of Christ. I am helped by many in my ministry for which I am grateful. Joined together we can accomplish all the will of God. Together we are a blessing to many people. It is a privilege to work with others in the Body of Christ sharing the Gospel in this world.

Develop Your Spiritual Senses

The Philippians letter was written from the Palace in Rome when Paul was imprisoned there for probably two months. Paul was kept in the lower portion of the prison that also doubled as the central sewage system for the city. The stench alone would have been enough to overwhelm a man. A month into his imprisonment, Paul, because he was a Roman citizen, was brought up out of this black hole and permitted to write a letter. This he did in his letter to the Philippians. In the letter he mentions the offering sent by the Philippians' Church to Paul by the hand of Epaphroditus. Though the stench of that awful prison was still in his nose, Paul could smell something else with his spiritual senses. But I have all, and abound: I am full, having received of Epaphroditus the things which were sent from you, an odour of a sweet smell, a sacrifice acceptable, wellpleasing to God. (Philippians 4:18). If we can develop our spiritual senses we can live above this natural realm. If we are to overcome the flesh and this natural sense realm we must live, walk and function in the spirit. We can by faith. By faith we can be more aware of the spiritual realm than we are of the physical realm. By faith we can SEE in the spirit: The eyes of your understanding being enlightened; that ye may know what is the hope of his calling, and what the riches of the glory of his inheritance in the saints, (Ephesians 1:18). We can HEAR in the spirit: He that hath an ear, let him hear what the Spirit saith unto the churches; To him that overcometh will I give to eat of the tree of life, which is in the midst of the paradise of God (Revelation 2:7). We can TOUCH and FEEL in the spirit: That they should seek the Lord, if haply they might feel after him, and find him, though he be not far from every one of us: (Acts 17:27). We can TASTE in the spirit: O taste and see that the LORD is good: blessed is the man that trusteth in him. (Psalm 34:8). How sweet are thy words unto my taste! yea, sweeter than honey to my mouth! (Psalm 119:103). And SMELL in the spirit: ....an odour of a sweet smell, (Philippians 4:18).

Developing God's Garden

The Word of God tells us that we are to think of ourselves and understand God's working in our lives just as we understand planting a field or a garden. 1 Corinthians 3:9 tells us, "For we are labourers together with God: ye are God's husbandry, ye are God's building." Husbandry is a word that denotes working with soil or land. We are the planting of the Lord. We are God's Garden. Our heart is the soil in which God plants the seed of His Word. The seed is planted by hearing the Word and the seed is nurtured, grows and develops in our hearts by speaking the Word of God. It is a fairly simple process. Plant the seed of the Word of God in the soil of our heart, nurture the seed, fertilize and water it by speaking the Word out your mouth. Continue to do so until the harvest. Jesus said, "For the earth bringeth forth fruit of herself; first the blade, then the ear, after that the full corn in the ear." (Mark 4:28). We must also work the soil by getting rid of rocks, weeds and thorns. In other words, deal with the things in your heart (the soil) that choke and hinder the planting of the Lord. For instance, "Take heed, brethren, lest there be in any of you an evil heart of unbelief, in departing from the living God." (Hebrews 3:12). Jesus also mentions that our hearts should not be filled with the wrong thing. And take heed to yourselves, lest at any time your hearts be overcharged with surfeiting, and drunkenness, and cares of this life, and so that day come upon you unawares. (Luke 21:34). We know how to plant the seed and nurture the seed but how do we deal with the soil? We are to remove unbelief by fasting and prayer. Jesus dealt with unbelief by teaching the Word. The prophets tell us to break up the fallow ground of our hearts by repentance and prayer. By doing these things the promises of God will find a place in our heart and we will begin to bear much fruit. Be sure the Word of God finds a secure place in your heart so that you may begin to see God's harvest of blessings in your life. Plant the seeds of love, faith and healing. Plant the seeds of prosperity and riches. God has a great harvest for you!

Divine Flow

There is a saying, "What goes around comes around." Or can I say it this way, "Whatsoever a man soweth, that shall he also reap." There is a divine flow of giving and receiving. This river of blessing flows from the throne of God and we are in that flow! And he shewed me a pure river of water of life, clear as crystal, proceeding out of the throne of God and of the Lamb (Revelation 22:1). There is a river, the streams whereof shall make glad the city of God, the holy place of the tabernacles of the most High (Psalm 46:4). God is the one who causes these waters to flow: He sendeth out his word, and melteth them: he causeth his wind to blow, and the waters flow (Psalm 147:18). I have found that as I have continued in this divine flow of giving, that God causes blessing to flow into my life. I do not want to do anything that will interrupt the flow of God's blessings into my life so I continue in the flow by continually giving. Get in the river and stay in the river! This is the divine flow of God's blessing!

Do Faithfully What You Do

Beloved, thou doest faithfully whatsoever thou doest to the brethren, and to strangers; 6 Which have borne witness of thy charity before the church: whom if thou bring forward on their journey after a godly sort, thou shalt do well: 7 Because that for his name's sake they went forth, taking nothing of the Gentiles. 8 We therefore ought to receive such, that we might be fellowhelpers to the truth (3 John 5-8). As this verse implies, John is thanking the churches for supporting workers (brethren and strangers), in the Truth who labored among those gentiles that did not cover their expenses and meet their needs. Those to whom we preach very often do not cover our expenses. Faithful friends and partners of our ministry have covered our expenses. This frees us to teach and preach wherever the Lord sends us. Because this is a biblical principal we can accomplish much. If we only received supply from those we minister to, our ministry would be severely limited. More often than not, I have ministered for those who could not or would not cover our costs to preach. Others have enabled me. Others have covered my expenses and the cost of ministry and because of this we have been able to accomplish much in ministry. If this had not been the case our ministry along with many other ministries could not complete the job at hand. I am a fellow helper of the Truth. I support the Gospel going forth. Anyone can have a great ministry by helping others preach the Gospel. I have traveled and preached through this nation and other nations by the help of others. In the open air, in prisons, in churches, under tents and in storefronts I have preached with Bible results because someone was a fellow helper of the Truth! On one occasion a pastor approached me and said that fourteen years prior I was preaching in a town in New England on the Canadian border. He told me God spoke to him in that meeting and he began to pursue the call of God on his life. He said that our meeting was the turning point in his life where he gave himself fully to the call of God. He had been in full time ministry for many years because of that one encounter. Lives are changed, bodies healed, deliverance and blessing are brought about because someone is paying for the Gospel to go forth.

Doing The One Thing

In order to be happy and have everything you want requires a simple formula. Discover God's desire. Want what He wants and He will give you what you want. F.F. Bosworth said it best: "Desire what God desires and desire it for the same reason He desires it and God will give you whatever you want." You can be happy and have everything you want! The rub is – it goes against everything in your flesh. Jesus said, "Deny yourself." In Matthew 16:24-26 it says, Then said Jesus unto his disciples, If any man will come after me, let him deny himself, and take up his cross, and follow me. 25 For whosoever will save his life shall lose it: and whosoever will lose his life for my sake shall find it. 26 For what is a man profited, if he shall gain the whole world, and lose his own soul? or what shall a man give in exchange for his soul? Similar passages are found in Mark 8:34-37 and Luke 9:23-26. Live your life with One Purpose and one goal. We all lead busy lives but we must focus in on the One Thing that is most necessary. One thing! What is the one thing? The one thing God wants from you is to reach out to those around you. Find a need and meet it. Refuse to satisfy your own desire so that you may satisfy the desire of someone else. If you can live this kind of unselfish life, everything will come to you; you will lack nothing, you will need nothing. Then Jesus beholding him loved him, and said unto him, One thing thou lackest: go thy way, sell whatsoever thou hast, and give to the poor, and thou shalt have treasure in heaven: and come, take up the cross, and follow me. 22 And he was sad at that saying, and went away grieved: for he had great possessions. (Mark 10:21-22). But one thing is needful: and Mary hath chosen that good part, which shall not be taken away from her. (Luke 10:42). Brethren, I count not myself to have apprehended: but this one thing I do, forgetting those things which are behind, and reaching forth unto those things which are before, (Philippians 3:13). Seek what God seeks and desire what God desires. But seek ye first the kingdom of God, and his righteousness; and all these things shall be added unto you. (Matthew 6:33). Knowing that whatsoever good thing any man doeth, the same shall he receive of the Lord, whether he be bond or free. (Ephesians 6:8). Do one thing today. Satisfy someone else's longing. Give joy to someone else. Meet someone's need. Do something good for someone and the Lord will repay you Himself!

Don't Be Discouraged

Follow the dream God has given you. Don't allow anyone to discourage you. If God has spoken to you, follow through. Go for it! Sometimes your opposition comes from those closest to you. They may not understand you or your dreams. That's all right. Forgive them and move on! Sometimes those you respect and honor disappoint. Those you trusted bring dismay. They will discourage you if you let them. You may find yourself in the midst of jealousies, strivings and contentions because of pride and hearts that are not pure before God. Always walk in love (smile and be sweet), toward the brethren but do not permit flesh, religion and man's ideas to thwart the plan of God in your life. You are accountable before God to fulfill His big plan. Be true to your own heart. Those who discourage you now will not be around when you must give an account to a Holy God. GO FOR IT! GIVE YOUR ALL FOR JESUS! HE WILL BE PLEASED.

Door To The Sheep

It is important to recognize variety of ministry in the Body of Christ. The Bible teaches that it is all the ministry gifts together that bring the Church to maturity. The Pastor is so vital to the Church. How we need good pastors in our churches! What a marvelous thing it is when there are anointed and equipped pastors in our churches. A Pastor over the flock of God is the doorway to the sheep. No one goes in or out without his consent and rightly so. He is there not only to feed and nurture the sheep but also to protect and guard the sheep. Even so, space must be given and allowances made for other ministry gifts to come into the local church. Paul explains that the Church requires not just the pastor's ministry gift but other gifts as well. And he gave some, apostles; and some, prophets; and some, evangelists; and some, pastors and teachers; 12 For the perfecting of the saints, for the work of the ministry, for the edifying of the body of Christ: 13 Till we all come in the unity of the faith, and of the knowledge of the Son of God, unto a perfect man, unto the measure of the stature of the fulness of Christ: (Ephesians 4:11-13). I honor and appreciate very much the pastoral gift. How vitally important it is! But the fivefold ministry is not made up of the pastor's gift alone. For a church to mature and be healthy, it requires other ministry. Without the influence of other ministry gifts, a church cannot grow and develop properly. The mystical church worldwide consisting of all Believers in Christ and the local church confined to one area both need a variety of ministry gifts. Can the church function with the pastor's gift alone? Many believe so but I cannot help but think that there will arise deficiencies and unforeseen difficulties. These are gifts. They do not have to be received but they certainly can be. They do not have to be accepted or used but if they are, the benefit is obvious. If an evangelist with the gift of healing is never presented to a church, only God knows who has been overlooked and missed out on heaven's best. Who knows what we have lost by not giving the itinerant teacher an occasion to deliver God's highest and best in the church. If the prophet or an apostle is not welcome only heaven knows what is lost. Where are the gifts of the Holy Ghost in the church? They come with the ministry offices. What has the Church lost by ignoring or rejecting the gifts that God gives? Who can tell? I say, invite them. Receive them. Embrace them. Who knows what amazing manifestation of heaven will come with a gift received. I thank God for those who have received my gift and opened a fruitful door of ministry. I know that Jesus will build His Church! And the gates of hell shall not prevail against it! I continue to offer my gift.

Elite Disciples

Jesus had those who followed Him throughout His ministry. There were significant differences in the followers of Jesus. We are most aware of the twelve who were closest to Him. They were learning and gleaning everything they could from Jesus which produced the phenomenal results we see in the book of Acts and all that took place in the early church. They were able to spend all their time with Jesus seeing and hearing the miracles that He did and listening to His teaching. Their lives were powerfully impacted. There was the twelve and beyond the twelve was the seventy. Jesus sent out the twelve and also sent the seventy to minister and preach the Gospel. These were ministering to multiple numbers of people. Then there was the multitude of people who followed Jesus to hear His Word and receive blessing and help for their lives. Many were healed, delivered and set free. Jesus ministered to the poor, brokenhearted, captives, the blind and bruised. His ministry was far reaching, touching a multitude of people. Many received from the ministry of Christ but there was an elite number who not only received from him but also gave back into His ministry and the Gospel. In order to touch the people that Jesus touched there were those who followed Jesus and supported His ministry. Some were helped personally; others were inspired by His message and recognized the significance of His remarkable life and ministry. They loved Jesus and they loved the Gospel. God stirred their hearts to support His ministry with their finances just as God stirs our hearts. A record of this is found in Luke Chapter eight, And it came to pass afterward, that he went throughout every city and village, preaching and shewing the glad tidings of the kingdom of God: and the twelve were with him, And certain women, which had been healed of evil spirits and infirmities, Mary called Magdalene, out of whom went seven devils, And Joanna the wife of Chuza Herod's steward, and Susanna, and many others, which ministered unto him of their substance. (Luke 8:1-3). Jesus was enabled, strengthened and supported by those who gave willingly and freely into His ministry. He was unconstrained in sharing the good news of the Gospel. These were elite disciples who received from the ministry of Christ and gave back so that others might receive.

Everybody Needs A Preacher

Traveling, preaching and ministering this glorious Gospel is my calling in life. This has been my focus for over 30 years now. The Gospel is the Truth and it is the only means by which people are saved, healed, delivered and set free. I say with Paul, I am not ashamed of this Gospel because it is the power of God unto salvation.... to everyone who believes. I preach His Word so that faith might come to people and they might believe and be saved. Paul clearly states the process of salvation in Romans chapter ten. For whosoever shall call upon the name of the Lord shall be saved. 14 How then shall they call on him in whom they have not believed? and how shall they believe in him of whom they have not heard? and how shall they hear without a preacher? 15 And how shall they preach, except they be sent? as it is written, How beautiful are the feet of them that preach the gospel of peace, and bring glad tidings of good things! (Romans 10:13-15). Everybody needs a preacher! Preachers are sent! Without a preacher people will not hear and if they cannot hear they cannot believe and if they do not believe they cannot call and if they do not call they cannot be saved. I have been sent to preach in order that people might hear, believe, call and be saved! We are going with the message... Preaching the Gospel of Jesus Christ.

Faith And Hope

If we understand how faith works we understand that we must have a goal out in front of us. Regardless of what it is you want, there must be clear vision and clear-cut goals for faith to work. Nothing is received without faith but in order for faith to work it must have a target. We see this from the book of Hebrews chapter 11:1. This is a superb definition of faith and shows us how faith works in a concise manner. Let's look at it. Now faith is the substance of things hoped for, the evidence of things not seen. (Hebrews 11:1). Faith is the stuff present in your life that shows you are hoping for something. The hope the Bible speaks of is not a hope so, maybe so type of hope. Bible hope is a definite event that is yet to come. Without a definite hope, faith has nothing to grab on to. Hope is a necessary ingredient for faith to work. You cannot have faith without hope leading the way. Hope is our goal and it is our vision. Hope is our confident expectation. Hope is the object of our believing. It is the thing we do not have as yet so we continue to hope for it. Faith, on the other hand is what is in your life today that will cause your hope to come to pass tomorrow. Faith is now. Hope will be there tomorrow. We must have hope and we must have faith. By these two things we receive what we desire. Hope by itself is wishful thinking. Faith without hope has no goals. It has nothing to shoot for. Faith and hope together accomplish the goal. I have the hope of touching our generation with the Gospel of Jesus Christ. My faith is what I am doing daily in order to see my hope become reality. I will do on a daily basis whatever it takes to reach my goal. The heathen, all the world, all nations and the uttermost part of the earth is our inheritance. I must preach this gospel in other cities also for thereto I am sent! I hope and I believe!

Faith Is An Act

Smith Wigglesworth, an evangelist from England in the early part of the 20th century said that faith is an act. In other words, faith expresses action. If we are to show God our faith it will be seen in our actions. Faith acts! I love the story of Naaman the Captain of the Syrian Host in 2 Kings Chapter five. He was a mighty man and valiant but he was a leper. A little maid, a servant girl to Naaman's wife mentioned that there was a prophet in Israel that could recover Naaman from his leprosy. Naaman wasted no time in contacting the king of Syria who in turn contacted the King of Israel, who contacted Elisha. Elisha's response was, "Bring him to me! He will know there is a prophet in Israel!" Shortly thereafter, Naaman shows up in front of Elisha's house. Elisha did not even come outside to chat but sent a messenger to tell Naaman to dip seven times in the Jordan River. Naaman nearly missed the prophet's instruction but after some encouragement by his servants, he obeyed the prophet's command. (Sometimes it takes a person with a different perspective to see things clearly). Naaman went and dipped seven times in the Jordan River and came up healed and cleansed of leprosy. Naaman did not allow any grass to grow underneath him. He was a man of action who got things done! The attitude, "If God wants me to have it then He will get it to me," does not work. This lazy man's approach will not get much of anything from God. Naaman was a mover and a shaker. He never allowed any moss to grow on his backside. Naaman had a faith that reaches out and takes. He moved out of his comfort zone and received all that God had for him. This is a faith that moves! This is a faith that acts! This kind of faith gets up out of the easy chair and pursues the promise of God. Move out in faith. There may be obstacles and hindrances but move ahead by faith. You will be glad you did! I am taking this Gospel wherever doors are open. I am walking in faith.

Faith Is Released

The Word declares that the just shall live by faith. If we are to live, as Christ would have us to live, we must live by faith. Faith is a product of the heart. (For with the heart man believeth; Romans 10:10). Proverbs 4:23 declares "Keep thy heart with all diligence; for out of it are the issues of life." Faith proceeds from our heart and the life we have in Christ is by faith as Paul said in Galatians 2:20, "I am crucified with Christ: nevertheless I live; yet not I, but Christ liveth in me: and the life which I now live in the flesh I live by the faith of the Son of God, who loved me, and gave himself for me." The life we live is a life of faith. Faith is released from our heart by what we say and confess out our mouth. Secondly, faith is released by what we see and continually look upon. And finally, faith is released by where we go and what we do. By your words, your vision and your deeds you determine how faith will be released through your life. Proverbs tells us exactly how to keep our hearts in verses 4:24-27: Put away from thee a froward mouth, and perverse lips put far from thee. -25 Let thine eyes look right on, and let thine eyelids look straight before thee. -26 Ponder the path of thy feet, and let all thy ways be established. 27 Turn not to the right hand nor to the left: remove thy foot from evil. Faith is released by what we say, what we see, and what we do. If we will pay attention to these three areas of heart expression we can develop a strong life of faith.

Faith Takes A Nap

And, behold, there arose a great tempest in the sea, insomuch that the ship was covered with the waves: but he was asleep. (Matthew 8:24). The obstacles we face in order to spread this Gospel are rendered powerless if we continue in faith. Jesus faced many obstacles as He went preaching. He was sought out by many. Some of His immediate family members thought he was deranged. Many misunderstood Him and others questioned His motives. The religious leaders of His day wanted Him dead and attempted to kill Him on more than one occasion. If that weren't enough, the devil tried to drown Him by a storm at sea. What was Jesus' response? He took a nap. Faith rests in the presence of a storm. Jesus has given us victory over all the power of the enemy. He may rant and rave but in the end the devil is defeated! Awakened by His disciples, Jesus simply spoke to the wind and waves to be still. Sometimes, the only action to take is no action. Get rested. Get some sleep. Then, when the time is right, speak PEACE to the problem and trust God to protect and watch over you. HE CARES FOR YOU!

Faithfulness Cannot Be Separated From Faith

Faith and faithfulness go hand in hand. Can we have faith for something and have it manifest immediately? I have had immediate answers to prayer but I still had to pray. The very definition of faith is to believe for something when you do not have it in your hands. Faith believes it has something before it can be seen, therefore faith must continue. Faith must be faithful. By faith and patience we inherit the promises. You can pray once but faith continues until the answer comes. Faith is faithful to confess the promise. Faith is faithful to do the Word. Faith is faithful to worship and praise God for the answer. When everything has been done, faith is faithful to stand on the promises of God.

Fight On!

In spite of tests, trials, difficulties and the attacks of the enemy, we are going to see this Gospel preached. We choose to fight on. Paul told young Timothy to fight. Fight people? No. Fight conditions and circumstances? No. Fight the devil and demons? No. Our fight is not with any of these things. Our fight is a good fight. Our fight is the good fight of faith. As Paul told Timothy: Fight the good fight of faith, lay hold on eternal life, whereunto thou art also called, and hast professed a good profession before many witnesses. (1 Timothy 6:12). There would be no fight of faith if faith did not have enemies. The arena of battle takes place in the mind. Paul alludes to this when he speaks of the weapons of our warfare. (For the weapons of our warfare are not carnal, but mighty through God to the pulling down of strong holds;) Casting down imaginations, and every high thing that exalteth itself against the knowledge of God, and bringing into captivity every thought to the obedience of Christ; (2 Corinthians 10:4-5). The Apostle Paul relates all kinds of challenges to his faith. Many were physical, that I am sure. Others brought extreme mental pressure. Paul was shipwrecked, once he was stoned, 3 times he was beaten with rods. He experienced hunger and thirst as well as frequent fastings and watchings. Not only that, because others loved him they counseled him not to be so intense. "Don't go up to Jerusalem, Paul!" Paul had to be true to His own heart. Some Bible teachers debate whether or not He should have gone to Jerusalem. Nevertheless he went. Was it a mistake? Who knows? God knows. I know this; Paul lived his life so as not to have any regrets. He made decisions based on how it would appear looking back from eternity. At the latter part of his life, Paul declares victoriously, "I have fought a good fight, I have finished my course, I have kept the faith:" (2 Timothy 4:7). These are the words of a man with no regrets. He fought the fight and enjoyed it. Though others quit before him he never surrendered to the assaults and attacks that came against him. He never stopped until he had reached his goal. He remained faithful to the mission and message God gave him. Continue fighting this good fight! Fight on!

For Saints And Sinners

This Gospel must be preached! We have good news to bring to saint and sinner alike. The Saints require a greater revelation of who they are and what they have. I often think if Christians only knew the authority they have, how different their lives would be! They need stirred up to lay aside weights and sin and go to a higher place in Christ. The Saints must be fed the good Word of God and encouraged in the Lord. They need a Word from God in due season! I believe God to be at the right place and at the right time to minister and strengthen the hands of Believers to get about the work of the ministry. Sinners need to hear the Gospel. They must hear. They cannot be saved unless they hear. I hope to see more saved, healed and delivered. I hope to see more lives changed! I hope to further my reach with the Gospel of Christ. This Gospel message is for everyone.

A Fresh Outpouring

We are living in the days of which Joel prophesied. These are the days that Peter proclaimed, quoting from the prophet Joel; 16 But this is that which was spoken by the prophet Joel; 17 And it shall come to pass in the last days, saith God, I will pour out of my Spirit upon all flesh: and your sons and your daughters shall prophesy, and your young men shall see visions, and your old men shall dream dreams: 18 And on my servants and on my handmaidens I will pour out in those days of my Spirit; and they shall prophesy: (Acts 2:16-18). Churches today are experiencing this outpouring of the Spirit. Those who are thirsty are pressing in to receive. Churches are preparing for a move of the Spirit in their midst. They are expecting it and making room for it! For those who are thirsty, God will pour out his Spirit. No matter your religious background or church denomination, if you are thirsty, you and your church can be filled with the Holy Ghost. It may take a while for a church to adjust, but once it does, the Holy Spirit has freedom to move in an unprecedented fashion. I say, "Make your Church a Holy Ghost Church." The need is enormous as I look across the spectrum of churches in America and Spirit filled Churches around the world. Many have left or neglected their spiritual roots and moved far away from Pentecost. I labor to see Pentecost explode in the local church. Everywhere I go people are filled with the Spirit. One here, five or six there, again and again people are receiving the Holy Spirit with the scriptural evidence of speaking in other tongues. Your day is coming. The Spirit has been poured out. The wave is rushing toward you! An understanding is coming to the Church. The Bible is an open Book! God is teaching His Church how to cooperate with His Spirit. When churches understand how to operate the gifts in an orderly fashion in the congregation, according to 1 Corinthians chapter fourteen, we will begin to see an abundant supply of the Spirit in the local church. With no exaggeration, not one church in 1,000 understands the proper use and order laid out in scripture. Few understand the place that the gift of divers tongues has in the public assembly. A lack of understanding about tongues and interpretation has nearly eliminated these signature gifts from the average church service. Because pastors and churches have not understood the proper order and operation of the gifts in the local church, these same gifts have ceased to function, even in many Full Gospel, Pentecostal, Charismatic and Spirit filled churches. We need a fresh infilling of the Spirit in our lives. We need a fresh move of the Spirit in our churches. I Believe to see a fresh outpouring of the Holy Ghost come to America and around the world.

Frustrating The Devil's Plan

In the Lord's Prayer Jesus mentions that we are to pray, "Deliver us from evil." And lead us not into temptation, but deliver us from evil: For thine is the kingdom, and the power, and the glory, for ever. Amen. (Matthew 6:13). Through daily communion with the Father we avoid mishaps and problems that we never knew existed. When we take the time to pray, we frustrate the devil's plan for our lives. His agenda is left unfulfilled and we permit the plan of God to be carried out. You have an astounding impact on the spirit realm through your prayers and faith! You make a difference! Your action in God makes a difference in the lives of countless individuals. You are an influence for God and for good! God has not forgotten your labor of love!

Fulfilling Desires

Thankfulness In the Body of Christ, being generous and being a giver go hand in hand with being a Christian. The result of being a giver can be seen in Paul's letter to the Corinthians: "And God is able to make all grace abound toward you; that ye, always having all sufficiency in all things, may abound to every good work: (As it is written, He hath dispersed abroad; he hath given to the poor: his righteousness remaineth for ever. Now he that ministereth seed to the sower both minister bread for your food, and multiply your seed sown, and increase the fruits of your righteousness;) Being enriched in every thing to all bountifulness, which causeth through us thanksgiving to God. For the administration of this service not only supplieth the want of the saints, but is abundant also by many thanksgivings unto God;" (2 Corinthians 9:8-12). What a great result! Supplying the wants of the Saints and creating thankfulness in the Body of Christ! Giving causes people to give thanks to God. This brings joy to the Father's heart to see His children caring for one another and sending the Gospel to a world that desperately needs it.

The Genuine Gospel

There are those who preach a form of godliness without the power. The Apostle Paul spoke of this to Timothy concerning the preaching of some: Having a form of godliness, but denying the power thereof: from such turn away. (2 Timothy 3:5). We are to preach and promote a Gospel of power. The genuine Gospel message delivers results. This genuine Gospel provides power to save, power to heal, power to live a holy life and power to change the lives of those who hear it and believe it. It's always a thrill to see someone lay hold on the Word of God allowing its power to transform his or her life. Salvation, healing, deliverance, miracles and infilling are the result of the Word of God preached with power. I am contending to preach this Gospel with Power!

Genuine Success

Daily we take up our cross to follow Him. Genuine success and prosperity comes by simply following Him. Two of my favorite scriptures are Joshua 1:8 and Psalm 1:1-3: This book of the law shall not depart out of thy mouth; but thou shalt meditate therein day and night, that thou mayest observe to do according to all that is written therein: for then thou shalt make thy way prosperous, and then thou shalt have good success. (Joshua 1:8). Blessed is the man that walketh not in the counsel of the ungodly, nor standeth in the way of sinners, nor sitteth in the seat of the scornful. 2 But his delight is in the law of the Lord; and in his law doth he meditate day and night. 3 And he shall be like a tree planted by the rivers of water, that bringeth forth his fruit in his season; his leaf also shall not wither; and whatsoever he doeth shall prosper. (Psalm 1:1-3). I am not talking about being religious or pious. I am speaking of knowing and following God. These two passages of scripture give us the key to a successful and prosperous life. We were created for God's purpose and He has a plan for our lives. In order for us to walk in the fullness of His plan we must focus on one thing: the Word of God. I am not speaking of daily devotions or going to church, I am saying all our thoughts, all day and all night are to be consumed and swallowed up in God and His Word. Everything we do has a touch of God. Every thought we think involves God and His Word. The obstacle to success in God is diversion. The Psalmist says it clearly. We can be blessed by simply avoiding the diversions. The three diversions he mentions are the counsel of the ungodly, sinners and the scornful (critics and criticism). If we simply avoid these there is a blessing. But it is not enough to simply avoid the wrong; we must focus on what is right and good. The good is the Word. Success does not come by dabbling in the Word with a little sprinkle here and there. No. Success comes by being baptized in the Word. Take a flying leap and go swimming in the Word! Our thoughts are saturated with His Word. God is in all our thoughts and meditations. As we live a life focused and consumed with His Word then His Word is infused to our being. We begin to fulfill what Jesus spoke of in John chapter 15: If ye abide in me, and my words abide in you, ye shall ask what ye will, and it shall be done unto you. 8 Herein is my Father glorified, that ye bear much fruit; so shall ye be my disciples. (John 15:7-8). Now we are living epistles. We are one with Him. His Word cannot be separated from us because it is thoroughly mixed into our being. The Word becomes part of our DNA. It is who we are. I want to bear fruit and be successful in all God has called me to be and do, don't you? I truly want to be His disciple. Then said Jesus to those Jews which believed on him, If ye continue in my word, then are ye my disciples indeed; (John 8:31).

A Gift Given, A Gift Received

Isaiah speaks of the greatest gift ever given: For unto us a child is born, unto us a son is given: and the government shall be upon his shoulder: and his name shall be called Wonderful, Counsellor, The mighty God, The Everlasting Father, The Prince of Peace. (Isaiah 9:6). We are able and willing to give because of the greatest gift ever given. Thanks be unto God for His unspeakable gift! The Father has given to us the phenomenal gift of His precious Son, Jesus Christ. It is my great honor to minister in many different churches. Very often pastors encourage me to take my liberty when ministering the Word of God. In other words, I am given the freedom to say what I want to say. This is a great privilege and I am careful to maintain proper etiquette and not overstep boundaries. Although we offer our services to whosoever will, not all are as willing to receive our ministry or give us their pulpit without reservation. Gifts can be given but they must also be received. Very often I have recognized the way I am received impacts how God moves in a service. On a number of occasions, because of a Pastor's willingness to receive the "gift" we offer, the Holy Ghost is free to show himself mighty in our midst. A beautiful operation of the Spirit of God is the result. All because the gift was not only given but "received" as well. It is evident that we have been given the greatest gift in the person of Jesus Christ yet many have not received Him though He has been presented to so many. A gift must not only be given it must be received. It is vitally important that we receive the gift that has been given. But as many as received him, to them gave he power to become the sons of God, even to them that believe on his name: (John 1:12). We have been given the greatest gift in the person of Jesus Christ. He is the greatest endowment ever made to the human race. We have redemption by Jesus Christ and the gift is freely given to all who will receive Him.   My prayer for you is that you might receive the fullness of the gift of God. I pray that your heart is enlarged to receive all that God has for you.

Give The Devil A Fit

It doesn't take very long running this Christian race to understand that we have opposing forces coming against us. The Good News is we have already won. We are more than conquerors, God always causes us to triumph in Christ Jesus and we have the victory through Him who loves us! Having said that we need to understand our enemies (plural). We must know our enemy. Someone aptly said the only problems you will have in this life would be from the devil and your relatives! I know what he meant, however our trouble stems not from those that are closest to us or people in general. Ours is a spiritual battle and a spiritual warfare. Even though it seems that people are the problem, the reality is there is a spiritual force at work motivating people. We are to love people (and our relatives) showing them the utmost kindness and mercy of God. Be gentle and loving toward people and direct you animosity and quarrel toward the devil. We have authority over devils and demons and the material world in general but we are not to rule over other men and women in the sense that we are domineering and controlling. The temptation is there of course but even God does not usurp a person's will or bring controlling forces against people. Witchcraft is essentially an attempt to control other people. People can pray and presume their will upon others and even though one may be praying, if they are assuming God's will for them, the prayer is wrong and it is witchcraft. Prayers not based on scripture, where we set the goals without listening to God are witchcraft prayers. In a witchcraft prayer we decide how a particular need is met. My prayer is always based on scripture and the revealed will of God. Where the will of God is unknown to me, I pray that a person comes to knowledge of the Truth and is established perfect and complete in all the will of God. Do not take your frustrations out on people. They are at times manipulated and motivated wrongly but people are not the problem. Paul saw this: For we wrestle not against flesh and blood, but against principalities, against powers, against the rulers of the darkness of this world, against spiritual wickedness in high places. (Ephesians 6:12). Our true enemies are the world, the flesh and the devil. When I speak of the world I am talking about this world system controlled by the god of this world, Satan and unregenerate men. It is a humanistic approach without God and without responsibility to God. This world's system through selfish and wanton disregard for people, has given us murder, war, abortion famine and disease. Pride, arrogance and the oppression of men are the result of this world's system. We are to put God first and worship Him alone. 100 percent of the world's problems would be solved if men humbled themselves under the mighty hand of God. Renew your mind so that the ways of the world do not hinder you, influence or break you. Our greatest weapon against a world gone crazy is to think like God thinks, see and understand the way God sees and understands and demonstrate the character of God at every juncture. Do this by living in the Word of God. Saturate yourself with the principles and ways of God. The world can't touch you when you are sanctified by Truth. Wherefore come out from among them, and be ye separate, saith the Lord, and touch not the unclean thing; and I will receive you, (2 Corinthians 6:17). Our second enemy is our flesh. We can resist the devil and he will flee but when you resist your flesh it stands and screams, "You want to fight? Let's get it on!" There is only one thing to do to your flesh and that is to put it to death. Water baptism represents death to the man of sin and resurrection to a new life in Christ. We are to present our bodies a living sacrifice to God. The problem with a living sacrifice is it tries to crawl off the altar every once in a while. Paul said concerning the body of his flesh: But I keep under my body, and bring it into subjection: lest that by any means, when I have preached to others, I myself should be a castaway. (1 Corinthians 9:27). So, how do we handle our flesh, the fleshly mind, actions and emotions? The simplest way to deal with your flesh is to oppose it. Your body wants to eat, make it wait and never give it as much as it wants. Your body wants rest so make it work another hour. Feeling angry? Don't kick the cat or give expression to the anger or emotion. Won't you explode, get an ulcer or have a nervous breakdown? Not if you are full of the Holy Ghost. Combat the flesh with the Spirit filled life and you will win over your flesh. Paul knew the power of the flesh. He said in Galatians: For the flesh lusteth against the Spirit, and the Spirit against the flesh: and these are contrary the one to the other: so that ye cannot do the things that ye would. (Galatians 5:17). How long do we war against the flesh? Until we put off the terrestrial and put on the celestial. One day we get a new body! Thank God I'm free. Free at last! Until then, fight the good fight of faith and don't give your flesh an inch. The final enemy we deal with is the devil, that old serpent. Satan, Beelzebub, Lucifer, the fallen archangel. There are only three things to do with the devil. Resist him (James 4:7); Cast him out (Mark 16:17); and give him no place (Ephesians 4:27). Don't listen to the devil, and don't let him do the talking. You do the talking. Say to the devil, "It is written. If he talks, say again, "It is written." This is the number one way to fight the devil. Know the Word and speak the Word and the devil will flee from you every time. Don't retreat and don't give up. Stay on the firing line. God is with you, God is for you and God is in you. You will win if you do not quit. Don't quit. Have faith in God. He will see you through to victory.

Give Yourself Away

Give yourself to others. Give yourself to God. There is great reward and reciprocal blessing in our giving. Paul, in so many words said that one could not out give God. He said that whatever we do for others God will repay us. With good will doing service, as to the Lord, and not to men: 8 Knowing that whatsoever good thing any man doeth, the same shall he receive of the Lord, whether he be bond or free.

(Ephesians 6:7-8). I look for places to give. The Word of God exhorts us not to be weary in well doing because in due season we shall reap. Payday doesn't come every Friday with God and it may not come at the end of the month but rest assured payday is coming! Godliness is profitable for the life that now is and the life that is to come. You will never regret any good thing that you've done for others. You will never regret any dollar you've given to promote Jesus Christ and His Gospel.

Giving Expresses God's Love

Around Christmas, I think of the greatest gift of all that we have in Jesus Christ. Our Heavenly Father is the original giver who has given us life and breath and joy and peace but most of all He has given us Jesus. "For God so loved the world, that he gave his only begotten Son, that whosoever believeth in him should not perish, but have everlasting life." (John 3:16). His love is indescribable and mind-boggling! The wonder of this gift of God's Son is that it is absolutely the best and greatest that God the Father had. Nothing else even comes close to this majestic gift! Because this is so, Our Heavenly Father has no qualms about giving us anything that is good and beneficial for you. Paul in describing God's overwhelming desire to bless us and give to us declares, "He that spared not his own Son, but delivered him up for us all, how shall he not with him also freely give us all things?" (Romans 8:32). Jesus Himself teaches that God shows us that He loves us by giving to us. "And in that day ye shall ask me nothing. Verily, verily, I say unto you, Whatsoever ye shall ask the Father in my name, he will give it you." (John 16:23). This terminology, "Verily, verily" literally means "I vow, I vow." It is the strongest thing that can be said to emphasize the fact that God the Father wants to give to us and bless us. God giving to us shows us in a very tangible way His love for us.

Paul declared in 1 Corinthians 13 that it is possible to give without loving but genuine love... the God kind of love... always expresses itself by giving.

The Goal

We continue to stretch our faith to reach out with this glorious Gospel. The Apostle Paul had certain goals in mind as he went to preach. He wanted to preach to those who had not yet heard the message of the Gospel. He would not rest until he had preached in what then was recognized as the whole known world at that time. He was also compelled to preach in Rome before Caesar. We hear Paul's heart to reach out as he writes to Timothy, Notwithstanding the Lord stood with me, and strengthened me; that by me the preaching might be fully known, and that all the Gentiles might hear: and I was delivered out of the mouth of the lion. (2 Timothy 4:17). Wow! That all the gentiles might hear! Paul continued in Ephesus at the school of one called Tyrannus and over the space of a couple of years he preached to multitudes! And this continued by the space of two years; so that all they which dwelt in Asia heard the word of the Lord Jesus, both Jews and Greeks. (Acts 19:10). Paul seeks to preach in Rome: After these things were ended, Paul purposed in the spirit, when he had passed through Macedonia and Achaia, to go to Jerusalem, saying, After I have been there, I must also see Rome. (Acts 19:21). And the night following the Lord stood by him, and said, Be of good cheer, Paul: for as thou hast testified of me in Jerusalem, so must thou bear witness also at Rome. (Acts 23:11). Throughout Paul's ministry, he preached wherever he found an occasion and sought out venues where he had never preached previously. Through mighty signs and wonders, by the power of the Spirit of God; so that from Jerusalem, and round about unto Illyricum, I have fully preached the gospel of

Christ. 20 Yea, so have I strived to preach the gospel, not where Christ was named, lest I should build upon another man's foundation: 21 But as it is written, To whom he was not spoken of, they shall see: and they that have not heard shall understand. (Romans 15:19-21). My goal is to take this gospel to any who will hear it. I know when they hear it and believe it; the Gospel will transform their lives.

God Himself

The blessing of Abraham belongs to us. What is the blessing of Abraham? We can find it in Genesis Chapter 15:1: After these things the word of the LORD came unto Abram in a vision, saying, Fear not, Abram: I am thy shield, and thy exceeding great reward. This blessing is to be bestowed upon the gentiles. That's you and me! That the blessing of Abraham might come on the Gentiles through Jesus Christ; that we might receive the promise of the Spirit through faith. (Galatians 3:14). What is it? God is our shield. He is our EXCEEDING great reward. It is God Himself. He has given himself to us. Notice that he said, "I am the God of Abraham, Isaac and Jacob. God literally gave himself to these patriarchs! Beloved, He has given Himself to you! Everything He is, Everything He has and everything He can do belongs to you! He is your shield! He is your reward. Himself! That is the blood covenant we have in Christ. All that He is, all that He has, all that He can do belongs to us!

God Is Not Finished With Us

Philippians 1:6 tells us, "Being confident of this very thing, that he which hath begun a good work in you will perform it until the day of Jesus Christ:" I know that God is not finished with us yet. He is working in us and through us to accomplish His will in the earth. God's Law of Sowing And

Reaping; and let us not be weary in well doing: for in due season we shall reap, if we faint not. (Galatians 6:9). The principle of sowing and reaping will work for you as long as you are doing what is necessary: 1. Sow your seed (give into the work of the Gospel) 2. Water and nurture the seed. (Speak the Word of God over your gift. Continue to praise God for His bountiful supply) 3. Wait for the harvest. (Don't get in a rush or lose patience Your harvest is coming. It is God's law and He will not fail!

God Is Our Source Of Supply

God is our source of supply for everything we need. Something I keep in mind is that whether gas is .50 cents a gallon or it is $5.00 a gallon He continues to be my source of supply. It is important that we remain in faith and trust Him in every situation. Remember to watch your tongue. It is easy to complain about prices. If we really see God as our source we will refuse to complain. To complain about prices is really to grumble and complain against God. It is as if we are saying, "God, you are not big enough to fill my gas tank." Remember, He is El Shaddai, the God who is more than enough. He is well able to take care of His children no matter what things cost. If we really believe and act in faith that God is our source we will begin to thank Him for His supply and care for us. Paul reminded the Philippians that God was indeed their source of supply and He would meet them. But my God shall supply all your need according to his riches in glory by Christ Jesus. (Philippians 4:19). David looked back over his life and made this observation: "I have been young, and now am old; yet have I not seen the righteous forsaken, nor his seed begging bread." (Psalm 37:25). He was chased down like an animal, faced battle after battle and at one point found himself living in a cave. Yet God watched over David. God protected

Him and God provided for him. God will do the same for you. He is a loving, caring Heavenly Father and He knows our needs even before we ask Him. We really do have a Heavenly Father who loves us and cares for us! Consider the ravens: for they neither sow nor reap; which neither have storehouse nor barn; and God feedeth them: how much more are ye better than the fowls? 25 And which of you with taking thought can add to his stature one cubit? 26 If ye then be not able to do that thing which is least, why take ye thought for the rest? 27 Consider the lilies how they grow: they toil not, they spin not; and yet I say unto you, that Solomon in all his glory was not arrayed like one of these. 28 If then God so clothe the grass, which is to day in the field, and to morrow is cast into the oven; how much more will he clothe you, O ye of little faith? 29 And seek not ye what ye shall eat, or what ye shall drink, neither be ye of doubtful mind. 30 For all these things do the nations of the world seek after: and your Father knoweth that ye have need of these things. 31 But rather seek ye the kingdom of God; and all these things shall be added unto you. (Luke 12:24-31). Rest assured, God will supply!

God Is Working In You

Successful ministry is not what we do but what God does in us and through us. It is what God is doing in our life and ministry. Whether big or small, it is God working in us to will and to do of His good pleasure. This is what Paul said: For it is God which worketh in you both to will and to do of his good pleasure. (Philippians 2:13). On one occasion I walked back to a man with heart problems and began to prophesy his healing. Previously the doctors had given him a gloomy report. He told me later after the prophecy that a peace came into his heart and he knew everything would be fine. A few days later he went to Pittsburgh for further testing and they could not find anything wrong. His heart was fit and strong! We continue to see God working in people's lives, healing them, saving them and filling them! A friend of mine recently asked me what my specialty in ministry is. I said "REVIVAL!" God is calling people to a deeper walk, a greater consecration. To receive all He has for us there must be a turning in our lives. True repentance. Repent and be saved, repent and be healed. Repent and be filled! Repent and receive His highest and best. God is working and God is doing through the Body of Christ. My prayer is that God does His work in me and through me to bless the Church and the world and that much fruit is the result. God working in and through others in the Body of Christ is the strength and encouragement of God. It is God working through you and others to will and to do of His good pleasure. You are God's vessel of love poured out.

God Speaks

Today we are ministering to many, many people through the spoken and written Word. Years ago the Holy Ghost spoke to my heart concerning our ministry. Although He has spoken many things to me throughout the years there are those things that stand out and the Spirit of God brings them to my remembrance time and time again. As I enter His presence in prayer or I ponder, "What is God saying," the things He has spoken rise in my spirit again and again. How do I know when God is speaking? How do I distinguish between God talk and other voices? Without going into great detail, God always speaks in line with His Word and with His character. If He has spoken something to you, He will remind you of it gently. God will not nag and annoy but He will persist until He gets His Word to you. When you are quiet, when you kneel to hear His voice, that thing He has spoken to you will be waiting for you. Before we actually began traveling to the extent we are today and before we had ministered the Word of God all over this nation and several other nations as well, the Holy Ghost spoke to me. In a time of worship and prayer the Spirit of God whispered to my heart in His own gentle way, "The lips of the righteous shall feed many." "The lips of the righteous shall feed many." "The lips of the righteous shall feed many." (Proverbs 10:21). Over and over He has reminded me that I am called and anointed to feed the Church Living Bread from heaven. Over the years countless thousands have been touched by the message placed in my heart by the Holy Ghost. This Word from God has been fulfilled and continues to be fulfilled, as we are faithful to the call He has placed on our lives. On another occasion while on an Indian reservation in New Mexico The Holy Ghost spoke a scripture reference to my heart. As I was laying in a missionaries' home in quiet meditation this scripture reference rose in my heart, "Zechariah 8:9." The Holy Ghost spoke and said, " This is for you." I opened my Bible to the reference and read; Thus saith the LORD of hosts; Let your hands be strong, ye that hear in these days these words by the mouth of the prophets, which were in the day that the foundation of the house of the LORD of hosts was laid, that the temple might be built. (Zechariah 8:9). As I thought on this scripture the Holy Ghost spoke again in my heart, "Son, I want you to strengthen the hands of Believers so they can get about the work of the ministry in order that my Temple might be built in the earth." Again and again we have brought encouragement and strength to those in the ministry and strengthened the hands of many that they might enter into their ministry. I am often reminded, "Strengthen the hands of Believers. Equip them with the things they will need for ministry." God is still speaking and I continue to feed God's people the Word of God and strengthen their hearts and hands to get about the work of the ministry.

God With Us

I have enjoyed nearly three decades of itinerant ministry. I preached my first sermon in 1977 and in 1980 I began pursuing the call of God on my life full time. I worked various part time jobs in those early years but my goal and purpose was to follow hard after the ministry God had called me to. I am so grateful for His guiding hand. He is always with us. Gwen and I have been through fire and flood and His grace is sufficient. He has blessed us beyond measure and He continues to bless us and load us down with benefits. I have four beautiful daughters and two beautiful granddaughters! I am thankful. I have learned though the years, "in everything give thanks". Circumstances may look bleak at times but I refuse to look at "lying vanities". The present condition may seem unchangeable but it is only God who is unchangeable. He is with us throughout our lives. He will never leave us or forsake us. Regardless of the circumstances, good weather or bad. The Word of God promises that He is with us. What does it really mean that God is with us? Well, let's think about it for a moment. God with us means we have the comfort of His presence. We have only to glance toward Him and we are reassured that He will never leave us or forsake us. God with us means that He is a very present help in time of trouble. There is no need to look to men for help. We have a friend that sticks closer than a brother. God is with us means that He is for us. He is on our side. Woe to any enemies who come against us. ...If God be for us, who can be against us? (Romans 8:31). God with us means we have fellowship with Him whenever and wherever. Where we go He is, whenever things change in our lives, He does not change. He is still there with us. God with us means He is watching over us. He looks out ahead of us. He protects us and forewarns us. God with us means He can talk to us. He can inform us and prepare us. God with us means there will be enough. God will provide. God with us means He will guide us and direct us. If we take a false step or make a wrong turn, He is still with us. He will lead us out. He will bring us in. God with us means we have joy. We have peace. We have love. God with us means there is no need to fear. There is no need to worry. God with us means we cannot fail! God is with us.

The Good Fight

We fight the good fight of faith in order to continue in the plan and purpose of God. This is the primary battle. Maintaining faith, right thinking and right speaking can be a challenge when circumstances and life's difficulties arise. We face trials and troubles that fly in the face of the scriptures and the promise of God. The battle is to maintain a victorious attitude in spite of present circumstances. God's promises stand sure but the challenge is to react in faith and not to our physical condition. In the natural, sickness and disease may ravage our bodies, the fight is to speak and declare the promise while the present condition prevails. My body tells me I'm sick but my faith declares that I am healed. (1 Peter 2:24). My body feels the pain and experiences the weakness but my faith shouts I am free! (John 8:36). I am healed! I am delivered by the blood of the Lamb! (Revelation 12:11). In the natural, the car won't start, the mortgage is due and the bank account is empty but my faith says that God supplies my every need! (Philippians 4:19), He has given me power to get wealth! (Deuteronomy 8:18), all things are possible to him who believes! (Mark 9:23), I refuse to worry because I have a heavenly Father who cares for me tenderly and affectionately

(1 Peter 5:7). Temptation threatens but God said He would deliver me from evil. (Matthew 6:13). He will not allow me to be tempted above what I am able to handle and will with the temptation make a way of escape for me! (1 Corinthians 10:13). The devil says.... but God hath said! The dilemma is whom will you agree with? Whose words will you repeat? Fight the good fight of faith! Declare what God has said! Let your conversation be without covetousness; and be content with such things as ye have: for he hath said, I will never leave thee, nor forsake thee. 6 So that we may boldly say, The Lord is my helper, and I will not fear what man shall do unto me. (Hebrews 13:5-6). Stand tall in this fight. He has given us everything we need to be victorious.

The Gospel You Hear

The Word of God works! I have observed over the years that you get what you preach. When I preach salvation, people are saved. When I preach the baptism of the Holy Ghost, people are filled with the Spirit. When I preach healing, people are healed. When I teach faith in God, people learn how to apply their faith. When I preach a positive, encouraging message, people are encouraged. Today, people continue to be saved, filled, healed, encouraged and strengthened by the Word we preach. Two things are important to see in my observations. Number one, you get what you preach. A church will never see anyone saved if they do not preach salvation. A church will never see anyone filled with the Spirit if the Baptism of the Holy Ghost is never preached. A church will never see anyone healed if healing is never preached. Let me say it again. You get what you preach. The second thing that I see is that it is vitally important to hear the right message. What is preached has an impact on people. What is heard has an impact on people. What you continually hear will eventually show up in your life. Jesus said, "Take heed what you hear". (Mark 4:24). Preach the Gospel and you will get corresponding results. Hear the Gospel and the Gospel you hear will show up in your life. Hear it and hear it again. Faith cometh. It comes by hearing. It comes by hearing and hearing and hearing and hearing by the Word of God. (Romans 10:17). Hear and be healed! Hear and be saved! Hear and be prospered! Hear the Gospel and preach the Gospel! Thank God for Good News. I say with Paul, I am not ashamed of the Gospel of Christ! (Romans 1:16). The preaching and hearing of the Gospel is the power of God to bring salvation to you! I continue to hear and preach this glorious Gospel.

A Grace Called Giving

Giving is an extraordinary spiritual key in our hands. I wonder sometimes if we fully understand the ramifications of our giving to God. Around the world the Gospel goes forth, hearts are gladdened and needs are met because of this marvelous grace called giving. Giving is the essence of a loving heart. One may give without loving but one can never love without giving. Loving and giving are so closely intertwined that it is difficult to distinguish one from the other. If we love with Agape: God's love, we will give. The essence of God is love. God is the great Giver. The Father's heart is a loving heart. It is a giving heart. There is not one life left untouched by the giving heart of the Father. The Father gives to all things living, life and breath. Because He loves, He gives. John in his epistle writes: We love him, because he first loved us. (1 John 4:19). Because we recognize, perceive and believe God's love to us, we love. God is our example in love. He is our example in giving. To love is to give: sacrificially, abundantly and unpretentiously. Be ye therefore followers of God, as dear children; 2And walk in love, as Christ also hath loved us, and hath given himself for us an offering and a sacrifice to God for a sweet-smelling savour. (Ephesians 5:1-2). The Believer who follows God, who has God as his example, will be a Giver.

Grace Is Given To Everyone

I have been called to a particular ministry as each individual in the Body of Christ is called. We each receive grace to do what we do. But unto every one of us is given grace according to the measure of the gift of Christ. (Ephesians 4:7). Regardless of what we are called to do or be there is not any calling or position that can function separately from the rest of the Body. Paul in his letter to the Corinthian Church explains the function of the Body of Christ. Even though we are different and operate differently we are brought together in the Body of Christ to carry out His will and purpose. But now hath God set the members every one of them in the body, as it hath pleased him. (1 Corinthians 12:18). We are many members with one purpose. Each of us has a particular grace and calling to fulfill. Just as a physical body interacts and works with all of its members so does the Body of Christ, one member affecting many members and many members affecting one. Now ye are the body of Christ, and members in particular. (1 Corinthians 12:27). I am keenly aware of others in the Body of Christ helping me to execute the will of God. As we minister to one another we are implementing His great plan and purpose. We are in the Body and together we are fulfilling His divine will.

The Grace Of A Willing Heart

If ye be willing and obedient, ye shall eat the good of the land. (Isaiah 1:19). Grace simply means unmerited favor.

This is favor and goodness that we do not merit or earn. It is grace toward us. I am constantly amazed at God's grace to supply our needs. As we have preached and ministered throughout the years we have seen God supply over and over again. I know Him to be Jehovah-Jireh. He is the Lord who provides. This grace toward us not only provides for our own needs but looks beyond our own needs to the needs of others. This grace has put within us a willing and gracious heart to give. I have seen through the years that there is such a thing as the grace of a willing heart. This is perhaps the greatest grace of all. The grace that releases what is in its own hand to supply the needs of others. I have shewed you all things, how that so labouring ye ought to support the weak, and to remember the words of the Lord Jesus, how he said, It is more blessed to give than to receive. (Acts 20:35). This is truly great grace. An example of this type of grace is found in the book of Acts at the outset of the Church, ...and great grace was upon them all. 34 Neither was there any among them that lacked: for as many as were possessors of lands or houses sold them, and brought the prices of the things that were sold, 35 And laid them down at the apostles feet: and distribution was made unto every man according as he had need. (Acts 4:33-35).

Grace To Serve

And God is able to make all grace abound toward you; that ye, always having all sufficiency in all things, may abound to every good work: (2 Cor. 9:8). Ephesians 2:8-10 tells us "For by grace are ye saved through faith; and that not of yourselves: it is the gift of God: Not of works, lest any man should boast. For we are his workmanship, created in Christ Jesus unto good works, which God hath before ordained that we should walk in them." One receives grace for one area of service and another receives grace for other tasks. Each one of us needs grace from God to do the work at hand. I thank God for the grace He has given to help us in the work He has called us to. His grace is for all that all might be blessed!

The Greatest Life Changing Force

Behold, a sower went forth to sow; (Matthew 13:3). The Word of God is unequivocally the greatest life changing force in the earth. Spoken with conviction, it will move individuals to accomplish the impossible. They will endure hardship, separate from family and wander as pilgrims simply because they esteem Holy Scripture dearer than anything this life can offer. I count it a great privilege to carry the precious seed of God's Word to needy souls. Through the years, we have had a mixture of experience preaching the Gospel. I have been threatened with bodily harm, shouted down drunks in my meetings and had tornado winds blow down my tent. I have been misunderstood, attacked verbally, lied about, talked about, lied to, stolen from and generally misused. In the process, however, I have also seen individuals gloriously saved, healed, filled with the Holy Ghost, forsake sin and enter the ministry. I have spit in blind eyes and seen them open, stuck my fingers in deaf ears and they hear, seen the lame walk and run and cancers disappear. I am always thrilled when the Holy Spirit shows up in our meetings revealing the secrets of men's hearts. I can hardly wait to see what happens next!

The Greatest Success In Life

I can remember going to Bible school as a young man out of high school and being awestruck by the dedication and sacrifice made by so many of the students. In my case, I was young and looking for adventure. It was my first extended time away from home and family. I was going to a place that would teach me the Bible, as few places would be capable of doing. The average age of a student attending the school was in their mid 40's. I was in awe of so many that had left home, family and careers to come to Bible School. There were doctors and lawyers and policemen who left their careers to come and study the Word of God. I had sacrificed a little but not like some who had left their careers and livelihood. Many brought their wives and children to an unfamiliar place to study the Bible. These had placed a premium on the Word of God. They were willing to give up everything in order to learn the scriptures and obey God. Jesus spoke of those who would be disciples of His: Then said Jesus unto his disciples, If any man will come after me, let him deny himself, and take up his cross, and follow me. (Mathew 16:24). This is any Christian's heart who is following Christ. As a teenager I read a book by Hall Of Fame running back, Gale Sayers, The book was entitled, "I Am Third". Sayers life philosophy is, God first, others second and ourselves third. (Sayers still holds the record for most touchdowns in his rookie season, most touchdowns in a single game, highest kickoff return average and most return touchdowns in a game Today he is known for his philanthropy and generosity. T.L. Osborne once said, "The greatest success in life is to find a need and meet it." If we can look beyond ourselves and begin to meet the needs of others we can find success and joy in life. My desire is to fulfill Matthew 16:24: Then said Jesus unto his disciples, If any man will come after me, let him deny himself, and take up his cross, and follow me. My life poured out for Christ and others. What is the result of a life poured out for others? For whosoever will save his life shall lose it: and whosoever will lose his life for my sake shall find it. (Matthew 16:25). I recently met an individual whom I had met nearly 30 years ago. His question to me back then was I just do not know what God wants me to do. Do you know what he said to me when I saw him again recently? I am trying to figure out what God wants me to do. I told him, "Find a need and meet it. Help someone do what they are called to do." If someone will do that, it will not be long before they are so busy they won't have time to wonder about what they need to do. Find your life by losing it in service and love toward others. Give yourself away. Follow Jesus with reckless abandon. Be a success. Find a need and meet it.

The Greatest Thing In The World

The Lord began dealing with me concerning my love walk. This is not a new revelation nor is it an unusual thing. It is simply loving God and loving people. The Lord was speaking to me. "Son, you want to see increase and blessing on your life, your family and your ministry, the one thing that is required is love for God and love for your fellow man. You stay in love and my blessing will be on you. Love me. Spend much time worshipping me. Exalt my Word, put my Word first place in your life. Show me that you love me." He went on to say, "Love people and be kind, be considerate, be courteous, be gentle. You are not missing it in the big areas. Take care of the smaller details." Being sensitive to The Holy Spirit and not grieving Him is so important. So many times we offend God and we are not even aware of it. We desire His blessing but we are like bulls in a china shop. We insult and offend God again and again and we remain totally oblivious to our errors. When we awake to righteousness and sin not we will be overtaken by His blessings. Likewise we ought to be sensitive toward people. Because of iniquity we have grown hard and callused toward people. What the world must see is the pure, unadulterated love of God flowing from our lives. This is the pinnacle. This is the greatest thing in the world that the love of Jesus be manifest to the world through you and me. This is what I want.

He Confirms His Word

The Word is working mightily! I am thankful that God has called me and allowed me to preach His Word! It is so simple! I preach and God shows up! Now, I am careful to preach the Word. Signs follow the preaching of the Word. He confirms His Word. Not my ideas not the world's news but His Word! I thank God for His Word. It is a saving Word. It is a delivering Word. It is a healing Word. I just returned from New York and we had a magnificent time preaching the Word of God. It was thrilling to see a lady who happened into our meeting. She came from across the street and was gloriously saved and filled with the Spirit. The Word works! I never tire of seeing lives healed and transformed by the Word and the Spirit! There is nothing so gratifying as seeing a life changed by God! And they went forth, and preached everywhere, the Lord working with them, and confirming the word with signs following. Amen. (Mark 16:20). We are taking the Word to hurting people. They are being healed, saved and delivered by His Word. I thank God for the Word.

Helped To Help

Where would we be if we did not have people around us who help? Some may have experienced a life that included very little help or maybe even those who should have helped them abused and neglected them. A life without help is the exception and not the rule. We are born being helped. Very few who give birth have had to do it on their own. The majority of us enter this life being helped! The average child is helped throughout his or her childhood. Parents, grandparents, baby sitters, teachers, coaches, instructors and friends have helped us all. All of us have benefitted from the "help" of others. As we reach adulthood we have years of lending a helping hand in our families, churches and schools. We are trained and encouraged to be a help to others. T.L. Osborn once said that the key to success is, "Finding a need and meeting it." I look for ways to add something to others, to be a help and encouragement to them. If we follow the Lord closely imitating Him, we will equip ourselves to be helpers. God is our great Helper and our example. He has promised blessing to those who "help" others. My help cometh from the Lord, which made heaven and earth. (Psalm 121:2). I am thankful for those who have helped me in life. Words cannot express what this help means to me. How can I do anything but be a help to others? The thoughts, prayers, actions and resources of others help me. I determine to be a help to others and I will live my life being helped.

Hidden Treasure

Again, the kingdom of heaven is like unto treasure hid in a field; the which when a man hath found, he hideth, and for joy thereof goeth and selleth all that he hath, and buyeth that field. (Matthew 13:44). I want you to see on the inside of me. I want to expose the inner workings of my soul. Why? Because within my heart, within my soul is a hidden treasure. It is the treasure of the kingdom of God. It is the treasure of Jesus Himself. There is a story in the Bible where Jesus tells about a man who discovered a treasure in a field. Once he discovered the treasure he sold everything he had to obtain the field because within that field he knew there was a great treasure. We are that field and Jesus is the hidden treasure. The Bible tells us that we have this treasure in earthen vessels. The treasure that I have to share with you is Jesus. The treasure that I receive from you is Jesus. I love the body of

Christ. Each member reveals another aspect of our blessed Savior. As for me, I want the world to see Jesus. Whatever I have of Him, I want to unveil and reveal to the world. My heart's longing and desire is to show Jesus to a lost and alienated world. I don't have all of Jesus and far be it from me to say that I have a full revelation of Him. No single person has a complete revelation of God. God fills the universe and the body of Christ is made up of many members. Eternity may not reveal the height and the depth and the length and the breadth of our Redeemer and his love. This being the case, I may not know or have all of Jesus but Jesus can certainly have all of me. Give yourself fully to Him. The more He has of us, the more of Himself He can unveil to us. I love him because he first loved me. I owe Him everything. As we go, people are saved, healed and filled with the Spirit. God has been gracious in giving us fruit for our labors.

The Highest And Best

Each of us in the Body of Christ make up a lifeline helping to carry out the will of God on the earth. God has an agenda. He has will and purpose. In Christ we have one purpose. We exist to fulfill His will and purpose in the earth. As we grow and mature in the things of God, we realize the will of God is the only thing that matters. In the scripture and throughout history, men and women have laid down their lives in order that the will of God might be done. One may wonder, what is the point? What is the big deal? And for those who are not acquainted with Him the question remains. But for those of us who know Him, who are familiar with His character, we can do nothing but fulfill His will. Jesus, in the face of the greatest challenge that God or man could ever face, surrendered Himself to the will of God. And he went a little further, and fell on his face, and prayed, saying, O my Father, if it be possible, let this cup pass from me: nevertheless not as I will, but as thou wilt. (Matthew 26:39). What lay ahead for the Son of God was almost too horrible to contemplate. The sinless Lamb of God bearing the sin of the world was separated from the Father three days and three nights. He faced unimaginable agony; still He accomplished the Father's will. Because Jesus pursued the purpose of the Father, many sons have come to glory. The Father has a family! You are in the family of God and I am in the family of God because Jesus was obedient unto death. He looked beyond the trial to the triumph. He endured the cross and shame to be seated in the highest place of victory. Looking unto Jesus the author and finisher of our faith; who for the joy that was set before him endured the cross, despising the shame, and is set down at the right hand of the throne of God (Hebrews 12:2). It is only our own shortsightedness that keeps us from walking headlong into the fullness of His will. What seems difficult or too great a price to pay is only an illusion. It is a lie of the enemy that there is any course that will benefit us more than the will of God. The highest and best for us is only one thing; God's will. I have determined that is the only course for me. Through the water; through the fire; through the storm; I will follow Him because I know the end from the beginning. I know the future is in Him and with Him. If He has made Himself known to you, if you have experienced His person, there is no other course for you other than the will of God. We stand together in the will of God. The highest and best for every Believer is the will of God implemented. My prayer continues to be... "Thy Kingdom come thy will be done."

His Eye Affects His Heart

God is our source of supply. When God spoke to Abraham concerning Isaac it must have been a traumatic event.

Think of giving up your own flesh and blood, your very own child! Yet Abraham knew that God had spoken to him. When Isaac asked what they would be sacrificing, Abraham replied: "... My son, God will provide himself a lamb for a burnt offering:" (Genesis 22:8). I love the wording of the King James Version. "God will provide himself a lamb!" Prophetic words that have been divinely fulfilled! Is it any wonder that Abraham is the father of all who believe? (Romans 4:11). Abraham knew the goodness and integrity of God. He was convinced that even though God required such a great thing that he was able to give back to him even greater. You see, God had already promised Abraham that in Isaac would his seed be called. He believed God to the point of resurrection from the dead! If he must offer up Isaac as a sacrifice he believed that God would raise him up! By faith Abraham, when he was tried, offered up Isaac: and he that had received the promises offered up his only begotten son, 18 Of whom it was said, That in Isaac shall thy seed be called: 19 Accounting that God was able to raise him up, even from the dead; from whence also he received him in a figure. (Hebrews 11:17-19). Abraham's faith was accounted as righteousness. The covenant of faith was sealed! Abraham offered to God all that he had. How could God hold back anything? Covenant says all that is mine belongs to you and all that is yours is mine. Abraham understood this in his covenant with God. At the place of sacrifice God revealed another aspect of His character. And Abraham called the name of that place Jehovah-Jireh: as it is said to this day, In the mount of the LORD it shall be seen. (Genesis 22:14). Jehovah-Jireh-the Lord who sees; the Lord who provides. The Lord will see; that is, God will do whatever is necessary for the nurture and provision of them who trust in him: hence the words are usually translated, The Lord will provide; God will provide; because His eye affects His heart, the needs and wants God sees in us He is ever ready and willing to supply. So we see this wondrous covenant sealed with the blood of Jesus! God's Son offered up. We can give freely because all that God has is made available to us through His Son! He that spared not his own Son, but delivered him up for us all, how shall he not with him also freely give us all things? (Romans 8:32). Are you in need? The Lord sees.

His Hands Were Heavy

Others strengthen me in the Body of Christ. Others help me in the Body. Others refresh me in the Body. I am not alone in battle. God is our help and He chooses vessels to bring into our lives. Those who can ease our burden and help carry our load. I cannot help but think of Moses as he stood before the armies of Israel with the rod of God in his hand. As long as he held high the staff, Israel prevailed but when he tired and the staff was lowered the enemy prevailed. When this became apparent, Aaron and Hur stood by Moses holding up his arms and so the armies of Israel went on to win their battle against Amalek. But Moses' hands were heavy; and they took a stone, and put it under him, and he sat thereon; and Aaron and Hur stayed up his hands, the one on the one side, and the other on the other side; and his hands were steady until the going down of the sun. (Exodus 17:12). What an amazing scene that must have been! What an astounding revelation this is! There are those who are holding up our arms as we run to the battle delivering living bread to dying men. Those who stand alongside of us help us take this Gospel message to humanity. I am grateful for those who hold my arms up high. I need help to win this battle. I want to hold up someone's arms. Their victory is my victory. If they are defeated it is my defeat as well. It seems like such a small thing to stand by another yet it is the difference between victory and defeat.

His Unspeakable Gift

When I think of the plan of God, to send His only Son. That all who believe might experience and enjoy ETERNAL LIFE, the ZOE life of God! Now we are Saved and Today we are Healed! Right now we are Delivered, Set Free, Prospered and Made Rich! Right here! Right now! We are blessed and happy! We have been given the greatest gift in Jesus Christ! We are Redeemed! We are in the Family of God! Jesus conquered and we are more than conquerors! No matter the problems you may have in the world. His Kingdom is inside us now! We have righteousness, peace and joy in the Holy Ghost! Thanks be unto God for his unspeakable gift. (2 Corinthians 9:15). JESUS!!! You have THE GIFT! Have faith in God! Have faith in the gift of God! I choose to focus on the gift! I choose to look at the Answer to all my problems. In fact there are no problems He cannot solve. With the Answer in my possession, I have no problems. I am glad that I have Jesus. I am glad that you have Jesus. He is the Answer! There is only One.

Holy Ghost Dependence

The Lord Jesus appeared to Maria Woodworth Etter and spoke to her concerning her ministry. She related this dialogue: "...Still I made one excuse after another, and Jesus would answer, 'Go, and I will be with you'... Then Jesus said again, 'Go, and I will be with you.' I cried, 'Lord, I will go. Where shall I go?' And Jesus said, 'Go here, go there, wherever souls are perishing.' My aim is to preach wherever souls are perishing. Only eternity will tell of the fruit that has been produced by Holy Ghost led ministry. We depend so much on the Holy Ghost. Jesus said in Acts 1:8, "Ye shall receive power after that the Holy Ghost is come upon you." In reality, there is no ministry without the Holy Spirit. We are effective because of the Holy Ghost. We have ability only by the Holy Ghost. We can attract people only by the Holy Ghost. The Holy Ghost will make you look good! We are a Holy Ghost Ministry. Thank God for the Holy Ghost! As best I can, I allow the Holy Spirit to have His way and accomplish what I cannot do myself. My job is to be filled and stay filled with the Holy Ghost. The infilling and operation of the Holy Ghost in our lives is the key to effective and powerful ministry.

Holy Ghost Manifestation

In one of my meetings I was preaching about the Syrophenician woman in Mark chapter 7. Afterward, a lady bowed her head and prayed silently, "Lord, if that woman could believe for her daughter to be delivered, I believe for my mother to be healed." When she finished her prayer I called out a word of knowledge by the Holy Ghost and told the woman's mother that she was being healed right then. A man who had been seeking the infilling of the Holy Spirit for seven years received and prayed in tongues all week long. He hadn't had a week like that for 40 years. In fact, he said he never had a week like that! Another man was determined that he would not fall down or be slain in the Spirit but after he and his wife came up for prayer they both were filled with the Holy Ghost and he fell like a bag of salt to the floor without anyone touching him! He hadn't had a good night's sleep for weeks but the very next day he told me he slept like a rock. The night before she came to our service, a young woman was praying about her future. She had questions about whether or not she would marry and have children. She cried and prayed, "Not my will Lord but thy will be done. I put my life in your hands."

The very next night I spoke a word of wisdom concerning her future husband and the children she would bear. This was a direct answer to her prayer the night before. Weeping, she began to rejoice and worship God. Another lady came forward for prayer. She had been experiencing stomach problems. I began to prophesy to her concerning her finances. She began to weep because she was in dire straits. I shared the Word of the Lord with her that her financial troubles were over. She began to weep and rejoice. A couple of days later she told me she had no more stomach problems and she hadn't a care in the world. Another lady received a Word from the Lord concerning the healing of her marriage and her husband's salvation. All week long people were born again, filled with the Holy Ghost and healed. This is what the Bible calls manifestation of the Spirit. (1 Corinthians 12:7). If ye then, being evil, know how to give good gifts unto your children: how much more shall your heavenly Father give the Holy Spirit (or Holy Ghost Manifestation). to them that ask him? (Luke 11:13). How do you get the Holy Ghost to show up? And I say unto you, Ask, and it shall be given you; seek, and ye shall find; knock, and it shall be opened unto you. For every one that asketh receiveth; and he that seeketh findeth; and to him that knocketh it shall be opened. (Luke 11:9-10). As I preach this glorious Gospel lives are changed. Our part is to pray and preach. When we do our part, God does His part and the Holy Ghost shows up in power. It is just that simple!

Honoring God

The promise of God is this: "for them that honour me I will honour, and they that despise me shall be lightly esteemed." (1 Samuel 2:30). When we make the effort to honor the Lord with our substance, He is ever vigilant to bless and reward accordingly. Men tend to neglect the spiritual side of life, and do not realize the affect their actions have on the invisible realm. God has made available to all an avenue of prosperity and blessing that literally is right in front of their nose, yet so many do not take advantage of it. Honour the LORD with thy substance, and with the firstfruits of all thine increase: So shall thy barns be filled with plenty, and thy presses shall burst out with new wine. (Proverbs 3:9-10). But seek ye first the kingdom of God, and his righteousness; and all these things shall be added unto you. (Matthew 6:33). Notice the words "firstfruits" and "first" in these scriptures. This is not just a passing thought to honor God this is an important priority. In fact, it is the first thing we do. When the things of God occupy first place, honor and blessing will be the "norm" for our lives.

How Many Oak Trees in One Acorn?

As for me, this is my covenant with them, saith the LORD; My spirit that is upon thee, and my words which I have put in thy mouth, shall not depart out of thy mouth, nor out of the mouth of thy seed, nor out of the mouth of thy seed's seed, saith the LORD, from henceforth and for ever. (Isaiah 59:21). Years ago while working at Rex Humbard Ministries in Akron, Ohio I was manning the phones for the ministry prayer and counseling department. I was on the night shift and early one morning I received a call from a woman who sang a prophetic word to me over the phone. The gist of the Word was that God was going to use me. She went on to say that she was seeing a vision of 3 pools of water each streaming into larger pools of water one below the other. She explained that the first pool and waterfall represented my ministry and the flow of blessing into the lives of the people I touched directly. From the second pool flowed a second waterfall that poured from the lives of people I had touched into a third, larger pool. This third pool represented the vast number of people touched and ministered to by the people I had ministered to. I understood by this vision the effect the Word of God has. When we give out to others, the blessing doesn't stop with them but multiplies and increases going on to bless many others. This is the principle that Paul explained to Timothy: Thou therefore, my son, be strong in the grace that is in Christ Jesus. 2 And the things that thou hast heard of me among many witnesses, the same commit thou to faithful men, who shall be able to teach others also. (2 Timothy 2:1-2). Be aware that you are having a greater impact than you know. Your influence and money does not end with your family and ministry but it continues on and multiplies again and again in the lives of those whom we touch. As someone aptly said "You can count the number of acorns on an oak tree but only God can count the number of Oak trees in one acorn." We are called to influence. We are called to be examples. Ministry continues to flow as water flows into a dry and thirsty land. I receive the flow into my life and in turn we flow out to others.

How Shall They Preach?

I have been ministering the Word with a fruitful return for many years now. The power of God has been present in our meetings to heal, save and deliver. The gifts of the Holy Ghost have been in mighty manifestation as we preach the uncompromised Word of Faith. I could do nothing without the generous financial help and prayers of others in the Body of Christ. Without the faithful support of others I could not do what I do. My ministry along with other ministries would be severely hindered. The Word must have free course. This message must be preached! Paul plainly said that Gospel workers must be sent. They cannot preach except someone sends them. Results and fruit begin with the senders.

Without senders nothing else is completed. The end result of a sender is someone calling on the Name of the Lord. Salvation begins with a Gospel sender. Everyone needs a preacher and preachers must be sent. For whosoever shall call upon the name of the Lord shall be saved. 14 How then shall they call on him in whom they have not believed? and how shall they believe in him of whom they have not heard? and how shall they hear without a preacher? 15 And how shall they preach, except they be sent? as it is written, How beautiful are the feet of them that preach the gospel of peace, and bring glad tidings of good things! (Romans 10:13-15). Without sending how shall they preach? Without preaching how shall they hear? Without hearing how shall they believe? Without believing how shall they call? Without calling how shall they be saved? Let the preachers preach!

How To Accomplish Anything

There is great power unleashed when we work together. What a person can accomplish alone is multiplied many times over by joining with others in a common cause. When the children of men set out to build a tower to the sky in defiance to God, they could have and would have done it had not God interfered with their plans. The principals for accomplishing anything are very simple. We see this in Gen 11:6: "And the LORD said, Behold, the people is one, and they have all one language; and this they begin to do: and now nothing will be restrained from them, which they have imagined to do." Within this verse we see five simple principals that will bring about any desired goal. Number one, the people is one- One goal, one mind, one purpose. Number two, One language- They are speaking the same thing and believing the same thing. Number three, This they Begin to do.- Nothing is ever accomplished until someone begins.

Number four, One imagination- They dream the same dreams and follow the same vision. There is one thing, however, that kept them from completing their plans. Their goal and purpose was outside of God's will and in direct conflict to the plan of God. So the fifth principal is that your goal must be in line with God's will. With these five simple principals a family, a church, a ministry or any group can accomplish anything. In this way, the Commission of Christ will be accomplished by having ONE purpose. Secondly, everybody involved speaks and believes the same thing. Thirdly, Begin. Nothing was ever accomplished until someone got started. Fourthly, dream, think and imagine one goal. And finally number five, our plans must be in sync with His great plan. In this fashion we will fulfill God's purpose and the Great Commission of Christ.

I Am A Debtor

Jesus Christ, our one and only Savior and Redeemer! I am often overwhelmed by the loving kindnesses and bountiful blessings of our Mighty Lord! Living wholly for Jesus we continually receive of Him. His Great love and Marvelous grace is lavished upon us. He has kept our heart inspired to keep on keeping on. As I receive these overflows of His goodness, I feel more and more like a debtor as the Apostle Paul put it in Romans chapter 1:14-15: I am debtor both to the Greeks, and to the Barbarians; both to the wise, and to the unwise. 15 So, as much as in me is, I am ready to preach the Gospel to you that are at Rome also. And also in Romans chapter 8:12: "Therefore, brethren, we are debtors," In an attempt to settle that debt of gratitude, I can do nothing but love, live, serve and be poured out for Him. As you experience the riches of His grace keep in mind that each of us owe a debt we cannot pay because of His great gift. There is no way to repay this debt but we can certainly acknowledge it! Our love, our worship, our giving and our service acknowledge the debt we owe. Never can we repay Him and still He continues to pour out upon us! And God is able to make all grace abound toward you; that ye, always having all sufficiency in all things, may abound to every good work: (2 Corinthians 9:8).

I Am Not Ashamed

I say with Paul, the apostle, I am not ashamed to preach the Gospel of Christ. It is the Gospel to us and it is the Gospel through us. It is the Gospel for our own help, salvation, healing and deliverance. It is the Gospel through us to minister to hurting and needy people. I am thankful for this glorious Gospel of Jesus Christ. For I am not ashamed of the gospel of Christ: for it is the power of God unto salvation to every one that believeth; to the Jew first, and also to the Greek. (Romans 1:16). I am not ashamed of this Gospel because it is the Word of God! I am not ashamed of this Gospel because it is a soul saving Gospel! I am not ashamed of this Gospel because it is a healing Gospel! I am not ashamed of this Gospel because it is an Eternal Gospel! I am not ashamed of this Gospel because it is a message that feeds my spirit! I am not ashamed of this Gospel because it is a message that cleanses my mind and heart! I am not ashamed of this Gospel because it produces faith in my life! I am not ashamed of this Gospel because it is joy to the world! I am not ashamed of this Gospel because it is peace to the world! I am not ashamed of this Gospel because the power of God is unleashed to me and through me! I am not ashamed of this Gospel because God is watching over His Word to perform it! I am not ashamed of this Gospel because it is good news for all who will believe it! I am not ashamed of this Gospel because it is a message that meets the needs of all mankind! I am not ashamed of this

Gospel because it is the sword of the Spirit! I am not ashamed of this Gospel because it solves the sin problem and no other message can do that! I am not ashamed of this Gospel because it is not another religion but reveals a relationship with God! I am not ashamed of this Gospel because righteousness is revealed! I am not ashamed of this Gospel because it is the TRUTH! I am not ashamed of this Gospel because it offers a new start and a new life! I am not ashamed of this Gospel because salvation is unveiled-healing, wholeness, soundness, provision and protection! I am not ashamed of this Gospel because I have embraced it and made it my own! I am not ashamed of this Gospel because it really does work! I am not ashamed of this Gospel because God confirms His Word with signs following! I am not ashamed of this Gospel because it is a Gospel of Hope! I am not ashamed of this Gospel because it is Light! I am not ashamed of this Gospel because it is life! I am not ashamed of this Gospel because it is my guide all the days of my life! I am not ashamed of this Gospel because it will turn this world upside down! I am not ashamed of this Gospel because it gives me power over the devil! I am not ashamed of this Gospel because it gives me power over sin! I am not ashamed of this Gospel because it has saved me from a devil's hell! I am not ashamed of this Gospel because it has made for me a home in heaven! I am not ashamed of this Gospel because it has filled me with the Holy Ghost! I am not ashamed of this Gospel because God really does love me! I am not ashamed of this Gospel because Jesus is the Author of it! I will preach this Gospel to all who will hear.

I Am Reminded

I thank my God upon every remembrance of you, Always in every prayer of mine for you all making request with joy, For your fellowship in the gospel from the first day until now;

(Philippians 1:3-5). Giving and receiving is a reminder of the goodness and faithfulness of God.

I Cannot Help But Give Again.

For unto us a child is born, unto us a son is given: and the government shall be upon his shoulder: and his name shall be called Wonderful, Counsellor, The mighty God, The everlasting Father, The Prince of Peace. (Isaiah 9:6). It is a joy to give with the understanding that God, our Heavenly Father gave to us the greatest gift of all, His Son, Jesus. When I think of what Jesus did for me, enduring the cross, despising the shame, dying for me, I cannot help but give again. I read of the lives of those who have gone before me, the precious apostles and saints of God who gave their all even unto death in order to keep the faith. They kept the faith for you and for me. When I ponder their lives poured out for the Gospel, I cannot help but give again. I look around and observe Christian workers laboring in churches and on the job giving a consistent witness, on mission fields, feeding the hungry and caring for the sick, I cannot help but give again. I gave my heart to Jesus as a young boy at Rex Humbard's Church in Akron, Ohio. A counselor led me to another room where I will never forget the elderly gentleman who explained the Gospel message to me as tears streamed down my face. I will always remember Mrs. Cordier who taught me to memorize scripture in my fourth grade Sunday school class. I learned the Ten Commandments, the Lord's Prayer, Psalm 100 and the 23rd Psalm under her tutelage. I will not forget the camp counselor who visited me in my home, laid hands on me and I was filled with the Holy Ghost with the evidence of speaking in other tongues. I often think of those who have ministered to me. I remember the youth workers, friends and pastors who gave of themselves to help me in my walk with Christ; I cannot help but give and give again.

I Cannot Out Give God

Our lives are dedicated and set apart for giving. God gave to us so how can we do anything but give back to Him? As much as I may try, I cannot out give God and neither can you. We continue to give and God lavishes His gifts upon us. He gave us Jesus and along with this His greatest gift He has given us everything. Do you need anything? Just ask Him. He has made it available to you. I love Him so much because He has shown His love to me. It makes me want to turn myself inside out to give back to Him. He that spared not his own Son, but delivered him up for us all, how shall he not with him also freely give us all things? (Romans 8:32). How can we do anything but give? And He has set it up so that we receive back more in abundance. He is a God of wealth and opulence. What a Savior! I am involved in the cycle of giving. We all are connected in the Body of Christ. We all feed one another. We all give to each other. I thank God for riches untold. This cycle of giving continues because we have received abundance from Him and we can do nothing but give in return.

I Continue To Preach

As an itinerant minister I have seen many people saved, healed and filled with the Holy Ghost. The Word of God has transformed countless lives. Those who are discouraged have been encouraged, those who are in doubt receive faith and those who have wandered are brought back to the fold. Jesus is preached and Good news is proclaimed. We have made a significant investment in taking the Word to people. We have given our whole lives to the preaching of the Gospel of Christ. We have traveled to preach in various and sundry locations with no guarantee of an income and no promise that our expenses will be covered. Very often we have borrowed money to preach, to travel, to reach people and touch lives knowing only that God supplies our needs. We have endured debt and lack in our personal lives in order to remain faithful to the call. I have done this for so many years now that often when things seem impossible and there seems to be no way to continue I know by experience that if God could do it one time, He can do it again. I know that God will come through for our family and ministry in some way, shape or fashion. I want to let the world know that Christ, our Savior was born and He died and He is alive forevermore! How will they hear unless someone preaches? How will they know unless someone tells them? We continue to preach and share this message of faith, hope and love wherever and whenever we have an occasion.

I Desire Fruit

Now ye Philippians know also, that in the beginning of the gospel, when I departed from Macedonia, no church communicated with me as concerning giving and receiving, but ye only. For even in Thessalonica ye sent once and again unto my necessity. Not because I desire a gift: but I desire fruit that may abound to your account. (Philippians 4:15-17). I desire fruit. So... Pray. Pray for an abundance of fruit. Pray for many to be saved, healed and filled with the Holy Spirit. Pray for mighty signs and wonders to be done in the Name of Jesus. Pray for boldness to speak the mystery of the Gospel. Pray for utterance in the Holy Ghost and open doors. Pray for divine favor with people. Pray that all financial needs are met. Pray because I desire fruit for you and for me.

I Give Myself To Prayer

ut I give myself unto prayer. (Psalm 109:4). David determined in the midst of conflict to give himself to prayer. Through the years when the challenges of life seem overwhelming, I have given myself to prayer. Thank God, He is there with us in the midst of trouble. There are trials that come where there is no one on earth who has the answer. God alone has the answer to our problems and God alone will hear and answer our prayer. Sometimes, people make a mistake by sharing their troubles with anyone who has a sympathetic ear. While counsel can be helpful and is needed and necessary at times, there are many areas of life in which only God has the answer and talking to more people may only serve to confuse the issue further. We have a Heavenly Father who cares for us and wants us to come to him for help. He above all else will provide solutions to the dilemmas of life if we will but pray. The Bible exhorts us to: Come boldly unto the throne of grace, that we may obtain mercy, and find grace to help in time of need. (Hebrews 4:16). Cast all our care upon him; for he careth for you. (1 Peter 5:7). Be careful for nothing; but in every thing by prayer and supplication with thanksgiving let your requests be made known unto God. (Philippians 4:6). If you are like me, many times, the troubles of life have forced my hand to prayer. But what victory there is in prayer! We can face life's dilemmas knowing that the answers are only a prayer away.

Identified With Christ

I praise God that we are identified with Christ! When you understand that it is no longer you that live but it is Christ that lives in us and through us we enter into His rest! We can face life with confidence knowing that we stand secure in Christ! We live by the faith of the Son of God. He is our life. He is our health. He is the one who stands facing the obstacles of life in us and through us. He is a conqueror. He is victorious. He is the One facing our enemies and fighting our battles. Jesus is for us. Jesus is with us. Jesus is in us. I am identified with Christ. I was buried with Him. I suffered with Him but praise God, today, I am raised up together with Him! I am seated with Him in heavenly places in Christ! Far above principalities and powers! In Christ I am a Conqueror! Through Christ I defeat all my enemies! My life is swallowed up in His life. It is impossible for me to be defeated! For me to lose, Jesus would have to lose. It is not possible for Jesus to lose! He has already won the victory for Himself and for me! I cannot go under for going over! I walk and live as a conqueror. The devil cannot touch me! For him to molest me, he would have to go through Jesus and the devil 'ain't goin' there! And having spoiled principalities and powers, he made a shew of them openly, triumphing over them in it. (Colossians 2:15). There is one who will fight our battles. He is on our side. The Greater One indwells us. He has made His habitation with us! I can face any enemy because He stands with me to defeat all them that seek to destroy me. I am in Christ today! You are in Christ today! Allow Him to live big on the inside of you!

Impacting This World And The Next

When the Gospel is preached, the seed of God's Word is sown and only eternity will tell the results. Even though God's Kingdom is about the invisible, a tangible seed sown produces tangible results. Lives are transformed, bodies are healed and the Church increases. Also, giving produces eternal fruit abounding in a heavenly account. When we give, we not only affect this present world but our influence goes on into eternity. Paul mentions this. "For even in Thessalonica ye sent once and again unto my necessity. Not because I desire a gift: but I desire fruit that may abound to your account."

(Philippians 4:16-17). "And God is able to make all grace abound toward you; that ye, always having all sufficiency in all things, may abound to every good work: (As it is written, He hath dispersed abroad; he hath given to the poor: his righteousness remaineth for ever. Now he that ministereth seed to the sower both minister bread for your food, and multiply your seed sown, and increase the fruits of your righteousness;). (2 Corinthians 9:8-10). What we do for God now in this time will impact our present world and produce eternal fruit that will go on into eternity.

In Everything Give Thanks

I spend time writing and sending thank you notes each month to express genuine gratitude to those who help me. I want to acknowledge those who have made a difference in my life. We are subject to so much negativity around us. People complaining, criticizing and grumbling never seems to wane. People complain about the weather, they criticize the government and they grumble about the economy. If these were all to their liking, they would fuss about family or just about anything else! Granted, things are not always as they should be or could be but one thing is for sure, we will never see anything change for the better by constantly complaining, criticizing and grumbling! Paul said this: Rejoice evermore. Pray without ceasing. In every thing give thanks: for this is the will of God in Christ Jesus concerning you. (1 Thessalonians 5:16-18). Being thankful is a way of life! It will mark everything we do! I want to set an example as a grateful person, don't you? I want others to understand that I am truly appreciative in regards to there influence and input in my life. Especially Him to whom we owe a debt we can never repay.

Included In The Work

The blessing of the Lord, it maketh rich, and he addeth no sorrow with it. (Proverbs 10:22). What an honor it is to give, to be generous and to bless with that which is in our hands. A child as soon as it understands there is work to do and a job to be done wants to be helpful. My granddaughters at 3 years old and 1 year old want to help their Mother with the dishes and with cleaning and whatever they can do. It is not that they are such a big help at that age but that Momma includes them in her daily chores. They are thrilled to have a part in getting the job done. I believe God puts that into each Christian at the new birth. We may not recognize it at first but within each of us there is the desire to be helpful, to take part and to feel needed in the plan of God and the Body of Christ. What a joy it is to come alongside of God the Father, our Lord Jesus and the Holy Ghost in fulfilling the great commission, winning the lost and making disciples of all nations. Could God do this without us? He's God, He can do whatever He chooses and He chooses to include us in the work of building the Kingdom of God and bringing in this "last days" harvest. What a thrill it is to be a part of what God is doing. Only God can save a soul, only Jesus can fill someone with His Holy Spirit. Only Jesus can bring divine healing, deliverance and wholeness to a person. Only God can do the work of God and He has chosen to include us in the work. How great is that? We are enabled by Him. We are equipped and prepared to come alongside of Him. With God we shall do valiantly!

Jesus Christ Is The Answer

And he said unto them, Go ye into all the world, and preach the gospel to every creature. (Mark 16:15). Jesus Christ is the answer. He is the answer to the world's problems. He is my Savior and the Savior of the world. What the world needs is Jesus. What governments need is Jesus. What business needs is Jesus. What the family needs now is Jesus. What the elderly need now is Jesus. What men and women, boys and girls everywhere need now is Jesus. Jesus is the answer to poverty, disease, crime, racial tensions and politics. Jesus is our answer! The Gospel means good news and the good news is Jesus! Jesus saves, heals, fills and delivers and Jesus is coming soon! Is their really a simple answer to the world's problems? Yes! His name is Jesus. Call on Him! Don't look at your problems look to your Answer. Your Answer is Jesus.

A Job To Finish And A Work To Be Done

And God is able to make all grace abound toward you; that ye, always having all sufficiency in all things, may abound to every good work: (As it is written, He hath dispersed abroad; he hath given to the poor: his righteousness remaineth forever. Now he that ministereth seed to the sower both minister bread for your food, and multiply your seed sown, and increase the fruits of your righteousness; (2 Corinthians 9:8-10). The reason that we are not taken on to heaven the moment we are born again is there is a job to be finished and a work to be done. We are here to develop and grow spiritually and do the work and will of the Father. What a joyous task is set before us. As we labor we are laying up eternal fruit. As we give, we are laying aside treasure for eternity. Our treasure can be found in the souls of men. Touching people is what ministry is all about.

Just Traveling Through

What powerful meetings we have had through the years. So many have been filled and healed! Over the years God has poured out His Spirit mightily in our meetings. Many have been saved, healed and filled with the Holy Ghost. Years ago the Lord spoke to me that our meetings would result in strengthening Believers and times of refreshing in the Holy Ghost. He gave me specific scriptures to believe and stand on: Thus saith the LORD of hosts; Let your hands be strong, ye that hear in these days these words by the mouth of the prophets, which were in the day that the foundation of the house of the LORD of hosts was laid, that the temple might be built. (Zechariah 8:9). Repent ye therefore, and be converted, that your sins may be blotted out, when the times of refreshing shall come from the presence of the Lord; (Acts 3:19). Churches and people desperately need a fresh deposit of the Spirit of God in their lives. There is a unique place that God has given evangelists, teachers, prophets and itinerant type ministries. I have been traveling in itinerant ministry for nearly three decades and I have observed Churches and Pastors as they relate to these Gifts in the Body of Christ. At times throughout history, because of a few unscrupulous individuals, itinerant ministers as a group have been looked upon with some foreboding and trepidation. In the early 20th century, Methodist and Holiness Churches made a move to ban traveling evangelists almost entirely from their churches because of the unscrupulous few. The result was that many churches moved toward a liberal theology and formalism and growth in their denominations leveled out and in some cases began to decline. The tide was turned, however, with powerful evangelists like Maria Woodworth Etter and Billy Sunday. Evangelist Billy Sunday was a fresh voice that stirred Churches and blessed entire cities with a simple Gospel message. Many were saved and delivered and His preaching against alcohol helped to usher in the era of prohibition. Etter had been preaching great revivals from the mid 1880's up until her death in 1924. She had to deal with persecution and misunderstanding as an evangelist and even more so being a woman in the pulpit. In the 40's and 50's a new wave of evangelism moved across this country. Pentecost and divine healing were brought to the forefront. Sadly, unprincipled evangelists and preachers disappointed and disillusioned many. There were also legitimate ministries embroiled in controversy that raised doubt and suspicion about the whole revival. Because of these things, this grand healing revival gradually waned and eventually disappeared. Following this were other movements, awakenings and revivals. All of these have had their share of criticism and controversy. The Jesus people of the 1960's and 1970's, the charismatic renewal, that impacted protestant and Catholic churches, the Word of faith movement of the 1970's and 1980's, the Toronto Blessing and the Brownsville revivals of the 1990's all made an impact. All of these received their share of criticism. Even to this present day this has been a pattern in the Church. In my quest to be a blessing and benefit to Churches, Pastors and their people, I have been misunderstood and approached with caution. Years ago I was interviewed on a Television Station that reached a Tri-State area and the interviewer began by talking about evangelists as a group being fraudulent and money hungry. It took me a little off guard and as best I could, I tried to bring some edification into the program, speaking about God's love and His heart toward a perishing world. I have sat in meetings and listened while other ministers have made light of, berated and accused gift ministries. It truly is pitiful! I realize that there are some bad eggs but that does not mean that we throw out the entire basket! Churches do a great disservice by rejecting ministries that are God given and Holy Ghost anointed. In some circles there is a trend, the pastor and internal ministry alone can satisfy every need of the church. This is a grave error. Churches may grow to thousands in number but without the variety of ministry gifts exposed to a congregation there are dimensions of spiritual life and growth that can never be attained by in-house ministries alone. There is a boldness and power that accompanies a gift ministry that is "traveling through." In our day, the itinerant evangelist, the televangelist and Internet preacher provide a tremendous aid to the local church. There is a deposit of the Spirit of God the church needs that can only come from these types of ministries. In truth, a genuine move of the Holy Ghost through a particular ministry may be embroiled in controversy. We should be very careful in our criticisms of such ministries. We see this from the inception of the Church. Let's look at the birth of the Church and the outpouring of the Holy Ghost in the Book of Acts. And they were all amazed, and were in doubt, saying one to another, What meaneth this? 13 Others mocking said, These men are full of new wine. (Acts 2:12-13). We see a pattern emerge that is unique to a true move of the Holy Ghost. First there is amazement people are awestruck. Secondly, people are perplexed and in doubt as to what is really happening. Thirdly, people become critical of what is happening. When there is a genuine move of the Holy Ghost amazement, doubt and criticism will follow. Throughout history, powerful preachers have been surrounded by controversy. We need these ministries that come alongside the local church. Controversy or no, God will use what is despised and misunderstood to bring help and blessing to His Church and a needy world.

Keep The Floodgates Open

Missionary Wayne Myers has a motto: His motto is "I live to give!" We are in the season of giving. If you are expecting a continual harvest there must be continual giving. The giving season never ends. At times you may think, "How can I give any more?" The very act of giving creates the return to enable us to give more. Stopping the gift stops the return. Continuing to give keeps the floodgates of heaven open so that we are able to receive abundance from Him. It is the exact opposite of what our natural mind thinks or what our flesh wants to do. God has set it up this way. There is an invisible world that responds to our good works and acts of kindness. By giving and honoring God we acknowledge His presence and blessing in our lives. I thank God in that He touched your life and you in turn are touching my life and in turn we reach out and touch a multitude of lives with the life and blessing of God. Giving is a great key. Continue the flow; continue to give because it will come back around to you in abundance! He is our example. He is the greatest of all Givers!

The Key To A Victorious Ministry

As I continue in ministry pouring out my life and giving of myself, there is always the temptation to draw back and withhold ministry and blessing from others. I have observed many who had much to offer but shut off the flow of God from their lives and became stagnant and embittered. Why does this happen? What are the dynamics of a good ministry gone sour? There are a multitude of sad stories in the Christian life. Many started out well and finished badly. There are so many with good and Godly intentions that never fulfill their destiny in God. They set out with high hopes and noble aspirations only to end up disillusioned and withdrawn. Why does this happen? I know that over the years in my Christian life and ministry I have been misunderstood, misused and misquoted. Like Moses of old, my good intentions were misrepresented and misread. As I have poured out the best God has given me in ministry to others I have gone under appreciated and unnoticed. The best that I have offered has been tossed aside and ignored. This is not reason to quit but an occasion to regroup and rethink. I have ministered the Gospel for years and I have every hope and intention of ministering many more years. How do we continue to serve God and give with joy and maintain a note of victory in the face of negative response and diabolic pressure? There is only one answer to that question and that is fellowship with the Father. Our only protection against offenses and demonic attacks is to dwell in the secret place of the Most High. We are to come again and again into the place of intimacy, abiding, and practicing the presence of God. If we will continue in His presence we can be steadfast, unmovable, always abounding in the work of the Lord. When we are faced with difficulties, situations that defy comprehension and people who abuse and misunderstand our good intentions, what are we to do? The answer is simple and straightforward. Run, don't walk but run to the bosom of the Father. He has everything we need. In that place there is peace; peace that passes understanding. In that place of abiding there is joy unspeakable and full of glory. In that place we meet the God of all comfort who comforts us in our distresses. Here is the Throne of Grace where we come boldly to receive help in time of need. This is the place where He is able to give to us above all that we can ask or think. I am resolved to continue my course with joy and triumphant victory. We overcome through Christ! Stay in the Secret Place. In this place, the devil, the world and even our own fleshly failings cannot win the day. Talk to Jesus. He understands. He is touched with the feeling of our infirmities. He will strengthen you. He will help you. In the Secret Place we win!

Knit Together

I am reminded that what I do I do not do alone. God's plan is that we depend upon Him and others in the Body of Christ. First of all, we are to put our whole trust in Him.

Second of all, we must realize that He uses people to accomplish His purpose in the earth. There is no place in the Body of Christ to say that we are "self made" or that we "pulled ourselves up by our own boot straps." Apart from Him we can do nothing. Isolated from the Body of Christ we can do nothing. Jesus clearly told us that this is the case. "I am the vine, ye are the branches: He that abideth in me, and I in him, the same bringeth forth much fruit: for without me ye can do nothing." (John 15:5). God has set it up so that we are part of one another and dependent upon one another. Throughout the New Testament letters to the churches we see that this is the case. God wants us to be aware that what we do, we do not do alone; what we accomplish is by Him, of Him and through Him alone and we do what we do through the Body of Christ. We are healed through the Body of Christ. Paul stated this in 1 Corinthians chapter 11. "And when he had given thanks, he brake it, and said, Take, eat: this is my body, which is broken for you: this do in remembrance of me." (I Corinthians 11:24). This certainly speaks of Christ's physical Body but also the mystical Body made up of Believers in heaven and earth. But let a man examine himself, and so let him eat of that bread, and drink of that cup. 29 For he that eateth and drinketh unworthily, eateth and drinketh damnation to himself, not discerning the Lord's body. 30 For this cause many are weak and sickly among you, and many sleep. (I Corinthians 11:28-30). We are to be considerate of the Body of Christ. James speaks of healing in the Body of Christ, "and pray one for another, that ye may be healed." (James 5:16). Peter says, "…. be ye all of one mind, having compassion one of another, love as brethren, be pitiful, be courteous:" (1 Peter 3:8). The writer of Hebrews tells us that we need those that have gone before and they need us. "that they without us should not be made perfect." (Hebrews 11:40). John tells us that love means interacting with people you can see. "If a man say, I love God, and hateth his brother, he is a liar: for he that loveth not his brother whom he hath seen, how can he love God whom he hath not seen? 21 And this commandment have we from him, That he who loveth God love his brother also." (1 John 4:20-21). We are a part of something that is bigger than ourselves. We receive what we do not deserve and we are members of a very exclusive group in which the only way to be a part of it is to die to yourself. Paul alludes to his dependence upon others in the Body again and again. Below are a few statements that he makes in his letters. "Ye also helping together by prayer for us," (2 Corinthians 1:11). "Brethren, pray for us." (I Thessalonians 5:25). "Pray for us:" (Hebrews 13:18). "We then, as workers together with him" (2 Corinthians 6:1). "Wherefore comfort yourselves together, and edify one another, even as also ye do." (I Thessalonians 5:11). "That their hearts might be comforted, being knit together in love," (Colossians 2:2). ".....from which all the body by joints and bands having nourishment ministered, and knit together, increaseth with the increase of God." (Colossians 2:17). "In whom ye also are builded together for an habitation of God through the Spirit." (Ephesians 2:22). Concerning giving Paul says, "For the administration of this service not only supplieth the want of the saints, but is abundant also by many thanksgivings unto God;" (I Corinthians 9:12). "Bear ye one another's burdens, and so fulfil the law of Christ." …."As we have therefore opportunity, let us do good unto all men, especially unto them who are of the household of faith." (Galatians 6:2,10), "For even in Thessalonica ye sent once and again unto my necessity. 17 Not because I desire a gift: but I desire fruit that may abound to your account. 18 But I have all, and abound: I am full, having received of Epaphroditus the things which were sent from you, an odour of a sweet smell, a sacrifice acceptable, wellpleasing to God. 19 But my God shall supply all your need according to his riches in glory by Christ Jesus." (Philippians 4:16-19). Prayer, Comfort, Completeness, Giving, Healing, ...all these come through association, affiliation and interaction. We function best together. We are part and parcel of one another. I am grateful to be a part with others. I am thankful for those in the Body who take part with me. Each person in the Body of Christ is a valuable and precious member. How blessed we are to have such a varied and sundry mix in the Church of our Lord Jesus Christ.

Knowing And Standing In The Will Of God

I count it a great privilege to preach the Gospel of Christ. I am aware that unless His hand was on my life I could not do what I do. And without others being obedient to God's plan I could not do what I do. I thank God for others obeying and fulfilling the will of God. We all could do our own thing. We all could go our own way. But what a satisfaction it is to know that we stand in the will and purpose of God. Paul prayed that we would know the will of God and stand in the will of God. This is my prayer for others and myself. It is my prayer for you as you read this book. For this cause we also, since the day we heard it, do not cease to pray for you, and to desire that ye might be filled with the knowledge of his will in all wisdom and spiritual understanding; (Colossians 1:9). Epaphras, who is one of you, a servant of Christ, saluteth you, always labouring fervently for you in prayers, that ye may stand perfect and complete in all the will of God. (Colossians 4:12). Pray and pursue the plan and purpose of God for your life.

Laborers Together

For we are labourers together with God: ye are God's husbandry, ye are God's building. (1Corinthians 3:9).

Ministering as a guest in a Church requires cooperation on many different levels. Many concessions are made for a guest speaker to come to a church or an area along with plans and preparations for the meetings. Some might say it's not worth the effort but if we are looking at things from God's perspective, He says it is worth it. Why is it worth it? When we do God's work, God's way things come together much easier. If a church is full of plumbers and a carpenter is needed to do a job it makes sense to call in the carpenter. There may be plenty of skilled plumbers but they do not have the necessary experience, tools and expertise to do the job a carpenter can easily do because of his training and expertise. So it is with the evangelist and itinerant teacher. They may not be able to do what a pastor can do but let them minister in their area of expertise and watch what happens. I preached at a church for an evening service years ago in northern Ohio. I preached the Word and began to minister to the people by the gifts of the Spirit. The word of knowledge and the word of wisdom began to flow. When I was finished with ministry, the pastor stood and told the congregation that what had been accomplished that evening in forty minutes time would have taken him six months of counseling in order to accomplish the same thing. We need skilled ministry to do the job at hand. Ministry working hand in hand with other ministry will get the job done. A principle that I have seen working over and over again is "Many hands make light work". What we accomplish alone is far surpassed by what we accomplish together. My goal is to assist in the work and ministry to which God has called others. Through God's help, it is a joy to add benefit and blessing to another ministry. I am not equipped to do what others do in ministry and they are not equipped to do what I do. But if we work together we get the job done.

The Least Of These

And the King shall answer and say unto them, "Verily I say unto you, Inasmuch as ye have done it unto one of the least of these my brethren, ye have done it unto me." (Matthew 25:40). As the years go by, I have come to understand that I am the smallest part of my own ministry. How so? Because it requires so many people doing so much in order for me to fulfill my calling. There are various individuals praying and giving to keep us going. Then there are those who provide opportunity and open doors. It takes an army of people to put one itinerant minister on the road. But even the least is important. If the least of these is removed, the ministry of all involved is ended. How necessary and needed is even the least! If the least and smallest is vital to the work of God, how crucial are the rest?

Liquid Properties Of The Word

Ho, every one that thirsteth, come ye to the waters, and he that hath no money; come ye, buy, and eat; yea, come, buy wine and milk without money and without price. (Isaiah 55:1). The Word of God is described as a liquid in this passage. A liquid has no definite shape and will acquire the shape of its container. In other words, the Word of God will fill us and be expressed through our personality. Also a liquid flows. It will go from the highest point to the lowest point and fill every nook and cranny. If the Word of God is allowed to flow freely it will affect everything it touches. In this passage of scripture the Word of God is like water because it sustains our life and without it we would die. We are clean by the washing of water by the Word! The Word of God is like wine because it cheers our hearts and causes us to rejoice. And the Word of God is like milk because it nourishes, strengthens and feeds our spirits. I say with the Psalmist, " O how love I thy law! it is my meditation all the day." (Psalm 119:97). Take time each day to drink of the water, wine and milk of the precious and powerful Word of the Living God! There is no other book like the Bible. We have the honor and privilege to pour out the Holy Scriptures to all who will receive it.

Living Life From The Inside Out

Over the years, as I have sought to serve God with all my being, the negatives in life have tried to rule the day. Paul describes what I have felt so often in 2 Corinthians 4:7-11. "But we have this treasure in earthen vessels, that the excellency of the power may be of God, and not of us. We are troubled on every side, yet not distressed; we are perplexed, but not in despair; Persecuted, but not forsaken; cast down, but not destroyed; Always bearing about in the body the dying of the Lord Jesus, that the life also of Jesus might be made manifest in our body. For we which live are alway delivered unto death for Jesus' sake, that the life also of Jesus might be made manifest in our mortal flesh." Paul contrasts the natural with the spiritual, the seen with the unseen and the carnal with the new man in Christ. It is important that we live our lives from the inside out. That we walk after the hidden man of the heart and not after the natural man. That we look on the inside where God is and not on the outside, and see only what our physical eyes see. The fourth chapter concludes with this verse, "While we look not at the things which are seen, but at the things which are not seen: for the things which are seen are temporal; but the things which are not seen are eternal." (2 Corinthians 4:18

Look For Reward

There is a definite reward for giving. When Paul was imprisoned in Rome the Philippians' church alone sent

Paul an offering. Paul rejoiced because God met his need through the Church at Philippi and there was a reward awaiting them. 15 Now ye Philippians know also, that in the beginning of the gospel, when I departed from Macedonia, no church communicated with me as concerning giving and receiving, but ye only. 16 For even in Thessalonica ye sent once and again unto my necessity. 17 Not because I desire a gift: but I desire fruit that may abound to your account. (Philippians 4:15-17). By taking part in God's great plan of giving and receiving, we meet the needs of people and position ourselves to receive greater blessing, reward and fruitfulness in life. I am confident that as I sow into God's purpose, believing, God's mighty hand of blessing is on me. I look for reward to come my way. I expect His blessing on my life.

Look On the Fields Of Harvest

Jesus said in John 4:35: "Say not ye, There are yet four months, and then cometh harvest? behold, I say unto you, Lift up your eyes, and look on the fields; for they are white already to harvest." We have only to look on the fields to see the great harvest of souls before us. The Word of God shows us to whom we are to minister. Jesus stood up in the synagogue and expounded on the harvest. The Spirit of the Lord is upon me, because he hath anointed me to preach the gospel to the poor; he hath sent me to heal the brokenhearted, to preach deliverance to the captives, and recovering of sight to the blind, to set at liberty them that are bruised, (Luke 4:18). More than ever we need to reach out to people. We exist to minister to the downtrodden, hurting and needy as well as those who seem to be self-sufficient. The Gospel we preach will make a difference for anyone who will believe it and receive it!

Look, Pray And Go

I know God blesses faithfulness. I have made every effort to operate our ministry with the highest standards. The Gospel of Christ is the message that saves, heals and delivers and it deserves no less than the best I can give it. The Lord spoke to me years ago to take His Gospel to the ends of the earth. His words were, "Touch every nation." I haven't fulfilled that dream yet but I'm not in heaven yet and I haven't quit! Each day we set our sights to live the dream. I believe that our greatest days of ministry are still ahead of us. I look at the condition of the world and I know it is our greatest time for harvest. Each day I pray and prepare is another step toward completing my course. As I go, I know God's purpose for me is to give a Word of hope, blessing and encouragement to people. What a glorious task lays before us! Our priority is to keep our focus. We are to look, pray and go. Jesus said it: LOOK: Say not ye, There are yet four months, and then cometh harvest? behold, I say unto you, Lift up your eyes, and look on the fields; for they are white already to harvest. (John 4:35). PRAY: Pray ye therefore the Lord of the harvest, that he will send forth labourers into his harvest. (Matt 9:38). GO: And he said unto them, Go ye into all the world, and preach the gospel to every creature. (Mark 16:15). To us who are intent on carrying out the Commission of Christ, Jesus tells us to look, pray and go!

The Lord Is Good To All

The Lord is good to all. We all experience so much grace... it is almost incomprehensible. But as Christians... those of us who are born into the family of God... we have a heavenly Father who cares for us dearly. He watches over us affectionately and is aware of all we need. The Bible is so very clear about his love for us. He does not want us to worry about anything, (Philippians 4:6). His desire is that we prosper and be in health. (3 John 2). He will not allow us to be tempted or tried beyond our capacity to handle it. (1 Corinthians 10:13). God loves us so! If we want something, He says Ask! And it shall be given! (Matthew 7:7). He has blessed us with all spiritual blessings in heavenly places. (Ephesians 1:3). Our Father has already looked ahead and prepared life and eternity for us. (Jeremiah 29:11, John 14:2). The whole world benefits from the love and goodness of God yet they do not acknowledge God nor are they thankful. Because that, when they knew God, they glorified him not as God, neither were thankful; but became vain in their imaginations, and their foolish heart was darkened. (Romans 1:21). I do not want to be numbered with them. I am thankful! I am very grateful to God the King. He is the giver of life and breath and all that we see and enjoy. God is good to us all and I will let the world know. Choose to be done with grumbling. Be done with complaining. We have a heavenly Father who loves us and cares for us deeply.

Love Is Greater Than All

And now abideth faith, hope, charity, these three; but the greatest of these is charity. (1 Corinthians 13:13). Under the tent a woman gave her heart to Jesus. The music is good with a different local group singing each night. The Holy Spirit has been giving me fresh messages each day. We are all enjoying the meetings. The crowds have been small (less than 50 most nights). but the Spirit has been abundant. I am glad for the liberty to preach and teach and minister to God's people. I preached a message entitled "Love is Greater Than All". I want to share the main points with you. Paul's great prayer in Ephesians 3:19 is that we might know the love of Christ which passes knowledge that we might be filled with all the fullness of God. I want to know Him and know His love. I want that love to come to me and flow through me, don't you? Love is the pinnacle of a holy life. Ability and talent may be developed in solitude but love and character is developed in the stream of life. Holiness is the love walk. Bible holiness can only be developed by interacting with people. Paul expresses this thought in his epistles. And the Lord make you to increase and abound in love one toward another, and toward all men, even as we do toward you: 13 To the end he may stablish your hearts unblameable in holiness before God, even our Father, at the coming of our Lord Jesus Christ with all his saints. (1 Thessalonians 3:12-13). Loving people will result in a heart unblameable in holiness before God. To walk in love is to live a holy life. But why is love the greatest of all? What is it about love that makes it the greatest thing? Love is the greatest because God is love. It is the greatest because love is the motivating force behind our redemption. (God so loved the world that He gave His Son).. Love is the greatest because it is evidence that we are born of God and have become new creatures in Christ. God's love is the greatest because by His love we are enabled to love others. In other words, we love because He loves us. Love is the greatest because it calls us out of the world to be sons and daughters of Almighty God. In other words, the love of God sanctifies and separates us. Love is the greatest because God dwells in those who love. Love is the greatest because when we love people, we know God in a greater way. Love is the greatest because it fulfills all the law of God. Love is the greatest because faith will only work by love. And finally love is the greatest because it is the mark of a perfect life. Jesus said be ye perfect even as your Heavenly Father is perfect. Jesus was inferring the Love of God. When we put on love it is the bond of perfection. I once wrote out 40 translations from 1 Corinthians chapter 13:4-8. These verses clearly define love. Not natural human love but Agape-God's love. 4 Charity suffereth long, and is kind; charity envieth not; charity vaunteth not itself, is not puffed up, 5 Doth not behave itself unseemly, seeketh not her own, is not easily provoked, thinketh no evil; 6 Rejoiceth not in iniquity, but rejoiceth in the truth; 7 Beareth all things, believeth all things, hopeth all things, endureth all things. 8 Charity never faileth: (1 Corinthians 13:4-8). If Christians walked in these verses, it would solve the majority of their problems. My sole purpose is to know this God of love and express that love to others.

Lowering And Lifting

Your part in the Body of Christ is important and significant. The epistles are full of comments on how we are to think of others and ourselves in the Body. The importance of each member is vital information for each of us. Never should we feel our part in the Body is overly important nor should we feel that we are insignificant. Two scriptures have meant much to me over the years as I relate to others in the Body of Christ. The first is found in Romans chapter twelve; Be of the same mind one toward another. Mind not high things, but condescend to men of low estate. Be not wise in your own conceits. (Romans 12:16). Condescend or lower yourself. Come down to where people live. When others are not in your social strata, leave your position and come down. Previously, in this chapter, Paul tells us not to think of ourselves more highly than we ought. How are we to think of ourselves? We are in Christ. We are kings and priests unto God yet we have nothing but what we are given. We are nothing but what He has made us. We are great because He has made us so! With this in mind, we ought to treat others knowing Christ has done or will do the same for all who come to Him. The second scripture is found in the epistle to the Philippians chapter two:

Let nothing be done through strife or vainglory; but in lowliness of mind let each esteem other better than themselves. (Philippians 2:3). In this passage, Paul encourages us to lift others to a higher position than we are ourselves. Esteem others better! Raise people and cause them to feel good about themselves! Nothing is worse than being in a gathering of people and being made to feel lower than those who are in the room. Lift people. Esteem people. I want to be around those who make an effort to relate to me whether lowering themselves or lifting me up. Those are the people I want to emulate and follow. Lower yourself and raise others. The ground is level in Christ Jesus. We are one in Christ!

Make Hay While The Sun Shines!

It seems the time just flies by! The older I get the faster it goes. The Word of God has much to say about time. What we do with our time and our attitude towards time is vitally important. For instance Moses mentions in the book of Psalms that we should consider that our days are limited in number. With this in mind we ought to make the best use of the time we have. In other words, "Make hay while the sun shines!" So teach us to number our days, that we may apply our hearts unto wisdom. (Psalm 90:12). In the New Testament Paul tells us to redeem the time. In other words, buy back your time for a good purpose and godly use. Make the best of the time you have. See then that ye walk circumspectly, not as fools, but as wise, 16 Redeeming the time, because the days are evil. (Ephesians 5:15-16). Having only so much time we need to prioritize our activities. If we do not prioritize we will find ourselves without enough time to do the most important tasks of the day. We ought to think in terms of not just what is needed and necessary but what is most important. Many things vie for our attention and time so we must put first things first. I am busy but I must put God first in my daily activities. I endeavor to spend time with God every day. Another priority that I have is my wife and family. Though many things are pulling for my attention, I must spend time with my family. John the Baptist preached so as to turn the hearts of the Father's toward the children. (Luke 1:17). In dividing up where we spend our time we must consider our priorities and their consequences. If I spend all my waking hours just pursuing the ministry with little or no regard for my family, eventually I would not have a family. If I only worked on ministry business, I would have no meaningful fellowship with the Lord. If all I ever did were pray, nothing else would get done. Understanding "First things first" is so important for a successful, victorious walk with God. Take time to evaluate and re-evaluate your priorities. When you put God first in your life, He will work out all the time details and cause everything to get done that needs done and you will be a lot further down the road.

Making A Difference

In Matthew 10:42, Jesus said, "And whosoever shall give to drink unto one of these little ones a cup of cold water only in the name of a disciple, verily I say unto you, he shall in no wise lose his reward." We sometimes put off a good deed, praying for or laying hands on the sick, giving, or witnessing because we feel our contribution is trivial or insignificant. It reminds me of the story of a little boy on a beach where thousands of small shelled sea creatures washed up on the shore and were dying. One by one the boy began throwing them back into the waters so they could continue living. A man walked by and said to the young boy, "Don't you see there are thousands of these little creatures washed up on the beach? What possible difference can you make?" The little boy continued throwing the creatures back into the sea and replied, "Well, Mister, it made a difference for that one."

Many Members- One Body

For as the body is one, and hath many members, and all the members of that one body, being many, are one body: so also is Christ. 13 For by one Spirit are we all baptized into one body, whether we be Jews or Gentiles, whether we be bond or free; and have been all made to drink into one Spirit. 14 For the body is not one member, but many. (1 Corinthians 12:12-14). The Church is a Body of Believers that functions similarly to a physical body. The physical body operates in a smooth flow of action, everything working together to accomplish its purpose. The simple act of throwing a ball includes direction from the head, the eyes, arms, and back, all the way down to the feet. Multiple body parts are involved in the simple act of throwing a ball. So it is with the Body of Christ. We are interdependent on each other in order that we might fulfill the will of the Father. God created us in such a fashion that we can accomplish almost nothing by ourselves.

Many Small Sacrifices From One Great Sacrifice

Although the Gospel is free to us it costs a great price. The initial cost was paid on Calvary when Jesus gave His life for a sin cursed world. Since then, many sacrifices have been made in like manner in order that hungry hearts might hear and receive this glorious Gospel. Paul the apostle relates his sacrifices to preach the Gospel. "Are they ministers of Christ? (I speak as a fool) I am more; in labours more abundant, in stripes above measure, in prisons more frequent, in deaths oft. 24 Of the Jews five times received I forty stripes save one. 25 Thrice was I beaten with rods, once was I stoned, thrice I suffered shipwreck, a night and a day I have been in the deep;

26 In journeyings often, in perils of waters, in perils of robbers, in perils by mine own countrymen, in perils by the heathen, in perils in the city, in perils in the wilderness, in perils in the sea, in perils among false brethren; 27 In weariness and painfulness, in watchings often, in hunger and thirst, in fastings often, in cold and nakedness. 28 Beside those things that are without, that which cometh upon me daily, the care of all the churches. 29 Who is weak, and I am not weak? who is offended, and I burn not? 30 If I must needs glory, I will glory of the things which concern mine infirmities." (2 Corinthians 11:23-30). By the ministry and sacrifice of Paul many were saved, healed and delivered and the known world heard the Gospel. Today, sacrifices are still being made that men might be set free through the preaching and demonstration of the Gospel of Christ. A gentleman came forward for prayer in one of our tent meetings. The doctors had not given him much hope. They said that he might only survive through the next six months or so. He had six stints in his heart to try and open clogged arteries but they had closed right back up again. One of his lungs was only partially working and the other was not functioning at all. He also had diabetes. After prayer I gave him the simple instruction to thank the Lord each morning that he was healed. He called me shortly after the tent meeting and told me that he had gone back to the doctor and after checking him thoroughly declared that he no longer had any heart disease or clogged arteries. Both lungs were functioning now and his diabetes was completely gone! Praise God forevermore! Sacrifice and ministry make this kind of result possible. How can I do anything but preach and minister this Glorious Gospel? Yes, I make sacrifices and give up some things but how can I do anything less in the light of His great sacrifice? It was Jesus who died for our sin and sickness that began the process.

Today, preachers, teachers and Gospel workers making small sacrifices daily to take this Gospel to the world... this results in deliverance, healings and salvation. Jesus saves, Jesus heals, Jesus is coming again! I am part of this process that began with His great sacrifice!

Meat And Potatoes

How important it is to preach and teach the basic fundamentals of the Gospel. I am a "meat and potatoes" kind of preacher. The message I preach will feed you and fill you. The Gospel really is simple. It takes help to misunderstand it. Religion has done a great job of confusing the issues. Paul was concerned that the Churches might stray away from the simplicity of the Gospel: But I fear, lest by any means, as the serpent beguiled Eve through his subtilty, so your minds should be corrupted from the simplicity that is in Christ. (2 Corinthians 11:3). Preach Christ and Him crucified. Preach Believe on Jesus and you will be saved from your sin. Preach the blood of Jesus and redemption through that blood. Preach the Love of God. God loves us. We love God and He has enabled us to love each other. Preach Salvation, healing and the Holy Ghost. Preach the Word. Thank God for the simple message of the Gospel. It will save to the uttermost. It will never grow old or become obsolete. This Gospel is forever.

The Mighty Word Of God

I know that the Gospel is the power of God unto salvation and if I have an opening to preach, the Word will have its effect. Paul conveyed the power of preaching and teaching the Word of God when he said: For this cause also thank we God without ceasing, because, when ye received the word of God which ye heard of us, ye received it not as the word of men, but as it is in truth, the word of God, which effectually worketh also in you that believe. (1 Thessalonians 2:13). The Word mightily works in those who believe it! Peter said it this way: Whereby are given unto us exceeding great and precious promises: that by these ye might be partakers of the divine nature, having escaped the corruption that is in the world through lust. (2 Peter 1:4) Jesus, just before He entered into the Garden of Gethsemane prayed for us and mentioned the life changing effect of the Word of God: Sanctify them through thy truth: thy Word is Truth. (John 17:17). Thank God for the Mighty, Mighty Word! Jesus is the Word. It's a Saving Word, it's a Healing Word, it's a Cleansing Word, it's a Blessed Word, it's The Word of God and Jesus is the Word! It's the Word of The Gospel, it's The Word of His Grace and it's the Powerful Word of God. It's the Word of Promise, it's the Word of Faith and it's the Powerful Word of God. It's the Word of reconciliation, it's the Word of Wisdom, it's the Word of knowledge, the Word of Truth, the Word of Life and it's the Mighty, Mighty Word of God. It's the Word of His power; it's the Word of righteousness, the Word of the oath, and the Word of My Patience. It is the Word of God that abides in you. For the word of God is quick, and powerful, and sharper than any twoedged sword, piercing even to the dividing asunder of soul and spirit, and of the joints and marrow, and is a discerner of the thoughts and intents of the heart. (Hebrews 4:12). We bare record of the Word of God! I love The Word. It has changed my life and I know it is mightily working in you!

Minister To Your Own Soul

We live by faith. Faith is a product of our spirit and our challenge is to always live in the spirit. The thing is, our soul (especially our emotions) and our body are vying for position to rule the day. Our soul is where the battle is and as the soul leans, so goes our lives. If our soul moves toward our flesh our bodies subdue us. If our soul leans toward our spirit, we walk in the victory of faith. Paul tells us this in the book of Romans, For they that are after the flesh do mind the things of the flesh; but they that are after the Spirit the things of the Spirit. 6 For to be carnally minded is death; but to be spiritually minded is life and peace. (Romans 8:5-6). As long as we are in our physical bodies on this earth, the battle wages between flesh and spirit. The key to maintaining victory is to keep our soul in agreement with our spirit. How can we do this? First, understand that this is an unending task. We will never ever be done with ministering to our souls. If we make it our business to maintain a spiritual mind we will always walk in victory. The simplest way I know to consistently minister to the soul is found in Paul's epistle to the Colossians: Let the word of Christ dwell in you richly in all wisdom; teaching and admonishing one another in psalms and hymns and spiritual songs, singing with grace in your hearts to the Lord. (Colossians 3:16). Throughout the day, sing the Word. Sing melodies you know and then make up your own. Minister to yourself in Psalms, Hymns and Spiritual songs. This I have found is the most effective means of keeping your soul filled with God's Word. Not only does this keep one filled with God's Word it also keeps us filled with the Holy Ghost! Paul in His letter to the Ephesians explains, And be not drunk with wine, wherein is excess; but be filled with the Spirit; 19 Speaking to yourselves in psalms and hymns and spiritual songs, singing and making melody in your heart to the Lord; (Ephesians 5:18-19). How Paul? How can I continually be filled with the Spirit? Speak to yourselves in Psalms, Hymns and Spiritual songs. Minister to yourself! This is the greatest way to minister to your emotions and keep your mind and thoughts on spiritual things. By singing faith building, Holy

Ghost uplifting and devil defeating songs you can stay on the victory side. We live in a negative world but we do not have to be negative. We can stay full of the Word of God and full of the Holy Ghost and maintain victory. I choose victory. How about you? I want to practice those things that will cause me to walk in success and triumph. Sing a God filled song today.

Ministry Of Giving

Paul the apostle wrote two thirds of the New Testament. His explanation of doctrine and care for the churches he founded fills his epistles. These churches also supported his ministry and Paul was not backward about mentioning giving and receiving in his letters. Paul's ministry depended on the financial support of those to whom he ministered. There is no New Testament ministry that can function at full capacity without the faithful ministry of those who pray and give. Thank God for this ministry of giving. Paul mentions giving over and over. Supporting and giving to ministries is a cornerstone of Christian faith and practice. Let me share with you a few instances where Paul mentions giving in the New Testament. I have shewed you all things, how that so labouring ye ought to support the weak, and to remember the words of the Lord Jesus, how he said, It is more blessed to give than to receive. (Acts 20:35). Our lives are to be filled with almsdeeds and giving. This is where great blessing resides! Or he that exhorteth, on exhortation: he that giveth, let him do it with simplicity; he that ruleth, with diligence; he that sheweth mercy, with cheerfulness. (Romans 12:8). Here Paul is speaking of a ministry of giving. (To give with simplicity literally means to give bountifully or with copious bestowal; to give generously) And God hath set some in the church, first apostles, secondarily prophets, thirdly teachers, after that miracles, then gifts of healings, helps, governments, diversities of tongues. (1 Corinthians 12:28). (The ministry of helps includes the ministry of giving). For ye know the grace of our Lord Jesus Christ, that, though he was rich, yet for your sakes he became poor, that ye through his poverty might be rich. (2 Corinthians 8:9). But this I say, He which soweth sparingly shall reap also sparingly; and he which soweth bountifully shall reap also bountifully. Every man according as he purposeth in his heart, so let him give; not grudgingly, or of necessity: for God loveth a cheerful giver. And God is able to make all grace abound toward you; that ye, always having all sufficiency in all things, may abound to every good work: (As it is written, He hath dispersed abroad; he hath given to the poor: his righteousness remaineth for ever. Now he that ministereth seed to the sower both minister bread for your food, and multiply your seed sown, and increase the fruits of your righteousness;) Being enriched in every thing to all bountifulness, which causeth through us thanksgiving to God. For the administration of this service not only supplieth the want of the saints, but is abundant also by many thanksgivings unto God; (2 Corinthians 9:6-12). Paul tells us this ministry supplieth the wants of the saints and many thanksgivings unto God! Let him that is taught in the word communicate unto him that teacheth in all good things. Be not deceived; God is not mocked: for whatsoever a man soweth, that shall he also reap. For he that soweth to his flesh shall of the flesh reap corruption; but he that soweth to the Spirit shall of the Spirit reap life everlasting. And let us not be weary in well doing: for in due season we shall reap, if we faint not. (Galatians 6:6-9). This speaks of ministering supply to those who feed you the Word of God. (Communicate means to give). But that ye also may know my affairs, and how I do, Tychicus, a beloved brother and faithful minister in the Lord, shall make known to you all things: Whom I have sent unto you for the same purpose, that ye might know our affairs, and that he might comfort your hearts (Ephesians 6:21-22). (Paul sends Tychicus to make known the affairs and needs of the ministry). Now ye Philippians know also, that in the beginning of the gospel, when I departed from Macedonia, no church communicated with me as concerning giving and receiving, but ye only. For even in Thessalonica ye sent once and again unto my necessity. Not because I desire a gift: but I desire fruit that may abound to your account. But I have all, and abound: I am full, having received of Epaphroditus the things which were sent from you, an odour of a sweet smell, a sacrifice acceptable, wellpleasing to God. But my God shall supply all your need according to his riches in glory by Christ Jesus. (Philippians 4:15-19). Charge them that are rich in this world, that they be not highminded, nor trust in uncertain riches, but in the living God, who giveth us richly all things to enjoy; That they do good, that they be rich in good works, ready to distribute, willing to communicate; (1 Tim 6:17-18). As we partake of this ministry of giving we receive back from God an abundant supply of the Spirit.

Ministry Of Reconciliation

Paul write in 2 Corinthians 3:6 that He has made us ministers of the New Testament. "Who also hath made us able ministers of the new testament; not of the letter, but of the spirit: for the letter killeth, but the spirit giveth life." While we are in this body there is a job to be done, a task to perform. We are to minister this New Testament to a world that has been alienated from God. The Old Covenant brought condemnation without righteousness. This New Covenant provides righteousness by faith without condemnation! We are to bring reconciliation to a world that has been alienated from God. 2 Corinthians 5:18-20 explains the ministry we have. "And all things are of God, who hath reconciled us to himself by Jesus Christ, and hath given to us the ministry of reconciliation; To wit, that God was in Christ, reconciling the world unto himself, not imputing their trespasses unto them; and hath committed unto us the word of reconciliation. Now then we are ambassadors for Christ, as though God did beseech you by us: we pray you in Christ's stead, be ye reconciled to God."

Moral Law Of God

In recent times men have sought to remove the Ten Commandments from the public square. This is not surprising because Paul said in the book of Romans that, "...they did not like to retain God in their knowledge." (Romans 1:28). Even so, this law has been engraved on man's heart. For when the Gentiles, which have not the law, do by nature the things contained in the law, these, having not the law, are a law unto themselves: Which shew the work of the law written in their hearts, their conscience also bearing witness, and their thoughts the mean while accusing or else excusing one another;) (Romans 2:14-15 Even though the moral law of God has been engraved on man's heart, in man's rebellion, he seeks to erase any evidence of the law of God in and around him. His foolish heart is darkened. Having the understanding darkened, being alienated from the life of God through the ignorance that is in them, because of the blindness of their heart: (Ephesians 4:18). Thank God, He did not despise the work of His hands but sent Jesus to reconcile the world back to Himself. Now, by believing on Jesus we fulfill the righteousness of the law. The law is preached (the ten commandments which is the moral law) to those who do not know God to expose their need for the Savior. It is by the moral law that sin is seen for what it truly is; sin. (...by the law is the knowledge of sin. Romans 3:20). The Ten Commandments show the sinner just how far He has strayed from God. After a man is thoroughly convicted of His sin by the hearing the law, it is at this point we can preach the Gospel of Christ so that he may be saved. It is evident that the world wants to erase any evidence of God from society. They do not want to retain God in their knowledge. We exist to spread the knowledge of God throughout the earth. We must continue to preach this glorious Gospel and give a lost world the opportunity to repent and believe.

More Important Than Money

. . . **m**oney answereth all things (Ecclesiastes 10:19). It would seem that money makes the world go round because without it, everything grinds to a screeching halt. Some would say that money is not important which would be synonymous to saying a 40 hour work week is wasted time. Money is important but it is not a goal to attain, rather, it is a tool to use. Money without divine purpose is unfulfilling at best. The Bible says, He that loveth silver shall not be satisfied with silver. (Ecclesiastes 5:10). To say that money is not important or that you do not care about money is not right either. To say money is not important is to say you do not care about paying your bills; you do not care about maintaining your house or car. To say money is not important is to say missionaries, evangelists and Christian workers are not important. It is to say the work of the local church is not important. All these things are important and necessary. And it is important that we take the money and resources God has given us to support and pay for God's work in the earth. Some have the idea that we are all in the ministry so full time, paid ministers are not needed. To believe that is to severely hamper and cripple the Kingdom of God in the earth. If I had to work a 40-60 hour secular job to pay my bills and then do all that I do in ministry, I can tell you, I would never be able to sustain such a schedule. Something would end up getting the short end of the stick. Either I would take more time to minister and my bills and family would be neglected or I would have to cut back on my ministry efforts and the work of God would be hindered and neglected. God ordains full time ministry. Do not misunderstand me. Through the years I have done whatever I had to do to have an effective ministry. Sometimes that meant working a full time secular job. Personally, I have never pursued any career but ministry. Out of high school I went straight to Bible school and my primary focus has always been the call of God and the ministry. That is not to say that I have not worked in secular situations. In fact, many of those secular jobs helped my attitude and perspective in the ministry. I have done whatever I have needed to do to develop and grow the ministry God has called me to and if that meant working a full time job I did it. As years have passed, I have become more and more centered and focused on this one thing that God has called me to. He sets in the church those who are called to minister before Him and to the people. If all we ever had were part time doctors, nurses, teachers, plumbers, carpenters, etc. etc., these workers would never be able to develop their skills, talents and abilities to the fullest. Paul said, "This one thing I do..." (Philippians 3:13). In order to do something well, all your focus and attention needs to be on that one thing. In one sense, many of us by necessity must be "jack of all trades" but if we are to shine at what God has created us to be and do, we need to pinpoint and laser in on exactly that. There is great benefit in being, doing and developing ONE thing in life. Whatever God has called you to, let that be your passion and purpose. Stay focused on that ONE thing and eventually the money and resources will be there to accomplish all that God has put in your heart to accomplish. Money is important but more important is the ONE thing He has called you to do. Money is simply a tool to help you do the One thing He calls you to do. Whatever you are called to do, stay with it. God blesses faith and faithfulness. You will walk in the fullness of your divine destiny. Help someone else pursue God's plan for his or her life. By helping others fulfill their calling, you move ahead in the plan of God for your own life. Pray for yourself and pray for others to move forward in God's plan.

The Most Effective And Efficient Activity

The most important aspect of our ministry is prayer. Our greatest effectiveness comes because of prayer. Prayer is first and foremost with our ministry. We are grounded on the Word of God following the pattern of the apostles as they gave us example. So prayer comes before everything else. Things were getting out of sync and out of order in the early days of the formation of the church. The Apostles found themselves involved in activities that kept them from doing their number one job. They stood up and declared what must be done. They restructured their lives to put things in proper order. Then the twelve called the multitude of the disciples unto them, and said, It is not reason that we should leave the word of God, and serve tables. 3 Wherefore, brethren, look ye out among you seven men of honest report, full of the Holy Ghost and wisdom, whom we may appoint over this business. 4 But we will give ourselves continually to prayer, and to the ministry of the word. (Acts 6:2-4). The result of putting things in their proper order was stated in verse seven of Acts Chapter six: And the word of God increased; and the number of the disciples multiplied in Jerusalem greatly; and a great company of the priests were obedient to the faith. (Acts 6:7). Prayer can be a challenge because there is always something vying for our time. One must also deal with thoughts that my time could be better spent in another activity. Prayer is the work that I give my time, effort and passion to. I constantly remind myself that according to the Word of God, prayer is the most effective and efficient activity I can involve myself in that will produce Bible results; i.e., the Word of God increasing, souls saved, filled with the Holy Spirit, healed and delivered.

Multifaceted Gospel

What does this good news Gospel consist of? I can speak of our eternal home in heaven or deliverance from sin. I can share that death and hell have no power over us. This good news Gospel includes the healing of our physical bodies and freedom from pain. We are redeemed from the curse of the law. We are redeemed from poverty, sickness and spiritual death. Not only are we redeemed from poverty but also He (Jesus) became poor that we through His poverty might be rich! The good news Gospel says that God has made us rich and by rich I mean a "full supply". This means having enough for our own as well as enough to give to others. We have all power over all the power of the enemy. Satan cannot touch us. He is a defeated foe. We have safety and protection because He has given His angels charge over us. The good news Gospel says He has a plan and a purpose for our lives. We were created and newly created for His purpose! This good news Gospel includes love, joy, peace and righteousness in the Holy Ghost. We have peace. We are filled with joy. Love and righteousness is our nature. We are new creatures in Christ. Old things are past and all things are new! We are forgiven and cleansed from sin by the blood of Jesus. Forgiven and cleansed! So much so that He does not want us to even carry with us a consciousness of sin. We are free from sin-consciousness and now we are free to develop a righteousness-consciousness. Not only all of the above is included in the good news Gospel of Christ but also all the promises of God are made available to us. From Genesis to Revelation the Word of God is filled with holy promises. Exceeding great and precious promises! Not one promise is held from us. By the Cross of Christ, through Jesus' death, burial and resurrection all these promises belong to us who believe. There is still one thing I have not mentioned concerning this Glorious good news Gospel. It is the greatest aspect of this Good News by far. That is, God is with us, God is for us and God is in us. Before the good news Gospel came to us we had no hope and were without God in this world. (Ephesians 2:12). As Believers we are with God and in Christ! We have relationship and fellowship with Almighty God! He is with us and we are with Him! He is with us by His Holy Spirit in the earth and we will be with Him for all eternity. To be absent from the body is to be present with the Lord! (2 Corinthians 5:8). Not only are we His children, we are His friends when we keep His commandments! (John 15:14). Abraham was called the friend of God along with all those who will cultivate their relationship with Christ. Every aspect of the Gospel pales in reference to this one thing. We are children in the Father's Family and we can know Him as Friend.

My Friend

I often think of the wonder and majesty of a God who created the heavens and the earth and all that we see and know who has come down to have a relationship and fellowship with men! What an awesome thing! What a privilege. We call Him Abba, (Daddy) Father! He cares for me! He loves me! He has a plan for my life! He is vitally interested in me and my family, my health and my prosperity.

He guides me daily. He is my Shepherd! He is the Master and Lord of who I am and what I do. What concerns me concerns Him. He watches over me tenderly and affectionately. I talk to Him everyday. I laugh and cry in His presence. He knows me. He understands me. He is a Friend who sticks closer than a brother. He corrects and chastises me but I don't mind because I know He loves me and it is for my own good. I love Him more than anything and my daily habit is to worship Him. He means everything to me! In Him I live and move and have my being! I am so grateful that I have a part and a place in the Body of Christ.

My Gospel

The Good News that Jesus is alive and still answers prayer is a powerful truth. In a sin sick, troubled and diseased world, the Gospel we preach provides solutions to a distraught society. I preached my first sermon in 1977 at 17 years of age. From that time until this, I am more convinced than ever that the preaching of the Gospel of Christ is the most effective means to alleviate the world's problems. Politicians are not solving the problems. Industry is not meeting the heart needs of man. Technology and science fall short of the real problems. Religion, corrupted by man's tradition has made a noble attempt but it is all in vain. There is only one answer to the world's dilemma. His name is Jesus. However simplistic and foolish it may seem, preaching the Gospel of Jesus Christ is the supreme method by which this world will be changed, one heart at a time. Because I am convinced of this, I continue to spend my life preaching the Gospel of Christ. I have given myself wholly to the Gospel. Paul said in 2 Timothy 2:8, "Remember that Jesus Christ of the seed of David was raised from the dead according to MY gospel:" Paul made it his Gospel. He loved the Gospel of Christ. Paul labored with it, suffered for it, and he gave up his life because of it. I say with Paul, this Gospel of Christ is MY Gospel.

My King

For God is my King of old, working salvation in the midst of the earth. (Psalm 74:12). David declared, "God is MY King!" Thank God we can proclaim along with David that He is MY King. He is MY Savior. He is MY Healer. He is MY Deliverer and My Provider. Thank God, Jesus is mine! I am so grateful for a personal Savior. The writer of Hebrews declares, "Let us therefore come boldly unto the throne of grace, that we may obtain mercy, and find grace to help in time of need." (Hebrews 4:16). He is very near to each of us. A very present help in time of trouble!

A Necessary Ingredient

Your obedience and faithfulness is making an impact for the Kingdom of God. You are a necessary Biblical ingredient in God's plan to get the Gospel to people. I don't know if you ever noticed but Paul's letters to the churches usually included something about their support of his ministry. He taught them the revelation that he had received from heaven and usually mentioned something about financial and prayer support of the ministry God had called him to do. We see in Romans, Paul saluted Urbane, his "helper" in Christ. (Romans 16:9). In 1 Corinthians, Paul gives instructions for the collection for the saints (1 Corinthians 16:1). In 2 Corinthians Paul exhorts that every man should give as he purposeth in his heart. (2 Corinthians 9:7). Paul mentions in the book of Galatians to let him that is taught in the Word "communicate" (or give) to him that teacheth in all good things. (Galatians 6:7). In Philippians Paul tells that particular church that God will supply all their needs by Christ

Jesus (Philippians 4:19). According to Paul, the church at Philippi was the only church that gave to him during that period. (Philippians 4:15). It is a joy for me to partner with others in spreading the Gospel of Jesus Christ. Lives are changed and people are impacted by this message. God has clearly made a way for His Gospel to go forth, we simply must work in cooperation with His plan to see to it that it does get preached and proliferated throughout the earth. I receive help to go forward with this Gospel message. We are serving up a gospel meal wherever doors open. We are doing our part to reach people. Others do the part to which they are called. The prayers and offerings of many are making a difference in the lives of individuals wherever the Gospel seed is sown.

Necessity Of Gospel Senders

There must be Gospel senders. The importance of sending forth those who preach, teach and minister the Word cannot be understated. Paul said in his epistle to the Romans: "How then shall they call on him in whom they have not believed? and how shall they believe in him of whom they have not heard? and how shall they hear without a preacher? And how shall they preach, except they be sent? as it is written, How beautiful are the feet of them that preach the gospel of peace, and bring glad tidings of good things!" (Romans 10:14-15). How will anything get done without those who send?

A New Day With The Promise Of God

Today is a new day. It is your first day. We begin a new day, a new week, a new month and a new year again! His compassions never fail! His mercies are new every morning! The past is done. It is over. Forget the past. Your future is bright with God's promises. Good things are in your future. We who believe are taking the promises of God into our future.

The promises of health, prosperity, wisdom and blessing go with us through the days, weeks, months and years. These are the exceeding great and precious promises for those who believe, for those who show God their faith. James said, "Show me your faith." (James 2:18). Rise up and show God your faith. Rise up and believe some good promise of God. Do something. Give something. Say something today! It is the first day of your future. It is a new day! I know the promises of God are for you and they are with you. You are blessed!

Night And Day Praying

Nearly every weekend I pack my things and head out to preach. Through the years many have been saved, countless others have been filled with the Spirit and healed. Times of refreshing come as we minister the Word and Spirit. I have traveled many roads and highways alone getting to the next place to preach. I have spent untold hours in my car, in airports and on airplanes. As I go, I pray for the meetings and pray for our partners and those whom the Holy Spirit brings to mind. Prayer could be the biggest part of my ministry. Prayer is vital to any gospel ministry. Paul understood the relationship he had with those to whom he wrote. They prayed for him and he prayed for them. Therefore, brethren, we were comforted over you in all our affliction and distress by your faith: [8]For now we live, if ye stand fast in the Lord. [9]For what thanks can we render to God again for you, for all the joy wherewith we joy for your sakes before our God; [10]Night and day praying exceedingly that we might see your face, and might perfect that which is lacking in your faith? (1 Thessalonians 3:7-10). Praying and preaching, I will never be done with it.

No Greater Love

I know that to be a giver involves sacrifice. As a father and a husband I lay down my life for my family because I love them. There is no greater love than a man giving his life for his friends. Jesus set the example for us in giving and sacrifice. This is love. Someone aptly said that you can give without loving but it is impossible to love without giving. Hereby perceive we the love of God, because he laid down his life for us: and we ought to lay down our lives for the brethren. (1 John 3:16). Greater love hath no man than this, that a man lay down his life for his friends. (John 15:13). I have been the recipient of sacrificial love. I have loved sacrificially. I am inspired and awestruck when I see this God kind of love demonstrated. I am thankful for those who love me with the love of God. When I am on the receiving end of loving and giving, I am then enabled to love and give to others. I want to continue in this cycle of sacrifice and giving. I want to experience sacrificial love in my life on both sides don't you?

No More Bad Days

Have you considered lately how blessed you really are? I am blessed! Every moment of every day, I am blessed! I stopped having bad days years ago. There are only days of blessing for me. Now wait a minute, trouble comes to every man. How can you not have a bad day in the day of trouble? I will tell you how. Trouble may come but I do not have to wallow in it. I can praise God in spite of it. I choose to be a worshipper of God. I choose to be thankful. I choose to be a worshipper in the midst of trouble. I acknowledge God in all my days and He only has blessing for me. This is the day the Lord has made. We will rejoice and be glad in it. (Psalm 118:24). What about trouble? This is how Habakkuk approached troublesome times. Although the fig tree shall not blossom, neither shall fruit be in the vines; the labour of the olive shall fail, and the fields shall yield no meat; the flock shall be cut off from the fold, and there shall be no herd in the stalls: 18 Yet I will rejoice in the LORD, I will joy in the God of my salvation.   (Habakkuk 3:17-18). I declare blessing! I decree happiness on you and in you by the Word of God. I choose to rejoice. I choose joy. I preach a Gospel of joy and victory. Let's receive it and walk in it.

No One Is Exempt

Maria Woodworth Etter, a salvation and healing evangelist, was known as the Grandmother of the early Pentecostal movement. Sister Etter had an incredible passion for the lost. Starting out in her fifties and preaching into her eighties, she crisscrossed this nation bringing salvation and healing wherever she went. In a vision, the Lord Jesus appeared to her and told her to go preach. Maria was born in 1844 in Lisbon, Ohio. I visited her hometown. In those days women did not even have the right to vote and preaching was something a woman would never consider doing. While looking upon Jesus in the vision, She told the Lord, "I will go but where shall I go?" Jesus responded and said to Maria, "Go here, go there, wherever souls are perishing." This is why the name of our ministry is Reach The World! As a preacher and teacher of the Word of God, I have no limitations as to where to preach. No one is exempt from this message! Jesus said, "Go into ALL the world and preach the Gospel (Mark 16:15). I go anywhere and everywhere unless He tells me specifically not to go to a certain place. This was Paul's approach to preaching. He went wherever an opportunity was afforded Him. At times he was kept from preaching certain places but he would just keep going until he had an open door! Now when they had gone throughout Phrygia and the region of

Galatia, and were forbidden of the Holy Ghost to preach the word in Asia, After they were come to Mysia, they assayed to go into Bithynia: but the Spirit suffered them not. 8 And they passing by Mysia came down to Troas. 9 And a vision appeared to Paul in the night; There stood a man of Macedonia, and prayed him, saying, Come over into Macedonia, and help us. 10 And after he had seen the vision, immediately we endeavoured to go into Macedonia, assuredly gathering that the Lord had called us for to preach the gospel unto them. (Acts 16:6-10). The whole world needs this Gospel. We are going on the wings of those who pray and give. I continue to preach the uncompromised living Word of God! Once I drove 10 hours to preach and 12 people were filled with the Spirit. This is what I live for.

No Small Decision

I am grateful for God's guidance and His mighty hand on my life. If we let Him, He will be our guide throughout our lifetime. Our lives are made up of small choices and small decisions we make on a daily basis. These are not insignificant because small decisions made consistently create lifelong habits and ultimately determine the direction our life takes. If we are familiar with scripture, many of our decisions are already made for us. Going to church, being a cheerful, generous giver, walking in love, etc. and so on will determine our outcome. God spoke to Joshua and said, "This book of the law shall not depart out of thy mouth; but thou shalt meditate therein day and night, that thou mayest observe to do according to all that is written therein: for then thou shalt make thy way prosperous, and then thou shalt have good success." (Joshua 1:8). What a great promise for knowing and applying God's Word in our lives! Concerning the daily decisions we make, how can we determine what is a good decision, especially if it is not particularly mentioned in scripture? Here are 5 guidelines for good decisions in life. First, when you are faced with a decision, ask yourself, "What does the Bible say about this? Find a scripture or scriptures that go along with what it is you are planning to do. If scripture plainly commands or disallows your plans there are no other steps. For instance, one need not pray about adultery, lying or murder. The answer is NO! You do not need a "leading to forgive someone or witness to someone. The answer is YES! Saturate your heart and mind with the scriptures. With a proper knowledge of the Word of God, you will successfully navigate the waters of life. Many decisions we make are not so clear-cut. So.... Secondly, make it a matter of prayer. God can work things out, circumstances, people, etc. He will give you peace concerning the matter or an uneasy feeling in your gut. You will become sensitive to your spirit man as you pray. It is important to follow this hidden man of the heart because you are born again and have the nature of God inside you. That along with a mind renewed with the scriptures is a recipe for success. It is a matter of being tuned in to the right frequency. The Third key to making good decisions is patience. Do not be in a rush to change direction. God leads us slowly and easily. Don't be rash. Take time to think things through. Have patience! Fourthly, follow your conscience. It is the voice of your recreated spirit. The human spirit trained in the Word of God is an accurate and safe guide. Your conscience will direct you in the right way. It will clearly speak, "Do this or don't do this." Finally, consider the consequences of your decision. If your choices benefit you but hurt those closest to you, that is something to consider. How will your decision today impact your health, your finances and your relationships? The decisions you make along with the words you speak will determine your future. Pause and consider the consequences of your actions. Do my choices in life honor God? Are my choices based on the Word of God? Will my choices produce peace and joy in my future? Allow every decision whether big or small line up with integrity and faith and your choices will bring you to blessing and honor.

On Schedule

The seasons come and go. I thank God that He is organized and He is always on time! It may seem late to us at times but God's timing is perfect! He said that as long as the earth remained He would keep us on schedule! While the earth remaineth, seedtime and harvest, and cold and heat, and summer and winter, and day and night shall not cease. (Genesis 8:22). Your seed sown into the work of God is a blessing where it has been planted and it will turn around and bless you again. God's promise is that as you sow consistently you will reap consistently. As you sow, God's plan is working and you will reap in due season. Have you sown in seedtime? Harvest time is coming. You can depend on it.

One Life To Give

The calendar flies by. If there is one thing I have seen through the years it is that time marches steadily onward. Jesus said work while it is day: I must work the works of him that sent me, while it is day: the night cometh, when no man can work. (John 9:4). As I grow older, I am conscious of the fact that I have one life to give to God and I must make the best of it. I must take the freedom that I have been given to win souls, preach the Gospel, teach people, be a help where I can and do what I must to take this precious seed of the Word to my generation. As I go about the task before me, I have come to recognize that time is my greatest treasure. While I have it, I must use my time for Him because the day will come for all of us when our time on this earth shall cease. Whereas ye know not what shall be on the morrow. For what is your life? It is even a vapour, that appeareth for a little time, and then vanisheth away. (James 4:14). The Lord willing, I shall complete the task before me. The moments, the seconds, minutes and hours given us cannot be wasted! Paul said in Ephesians, redeem the time. See then that ye walk circumspectly, not as fools, but as wise, 16 Redeeming the time, because the days are evil. (Ephesians 5:15-16). Redeem the time. Buy it back! Make up the minutes and hours that have been lost. Make wise use of moments and occasions for doing good. To redeem is to recover from the power of another. So take back your time and use it for God. Moses' prayer in Psalm 90 included: So teach us to number our days, that we may apply our hearts unto wisdom. (Psalm 90:12). Moses was aware that the clock was ticking. We must use the time we have for the things that matter. We run to take the Gospel of Jesus Christ to our nation and the world.

One Person

You are taking up the slack where others have failed. Paul, in his letter to the Philippians states it plainly: "Now ye Philippians know also, that in the beginning of the gospel, when I departed from Macedonia, no church communicated with me as concerning giving and receiving, but ye only. 16 For even in Thessalonica ye sent once and again unto my necessity." (Philippians 4:15-16). While Paul was in prison in Rome, there was only one church that remembered him and sent an offering to meet his need. One person or church can make a difference.

Open Doors And Open Arms

I always appreciate open doors and open arms. Someone aptly has said, "Go where you are celebrated and not where you are simply tolerated." To be received, accepted and made to feel a part with someone else is one of the greatest joys in life. I am always elated when others receive my gifting and ministry. Along with being received is the blessing that comes from receiving others. If we can accept it, there are hidden treasures in people that will enlighten and enliven our lives. Take down the barriers. Open your heart to receive the gift that has the ability to revolutionize your life. Everyone benefits when we recognize the Body of Christ and the variety of gifts in it. To be received by others is an amazing thing. A healthy and growing church recognizes the importance and value of other anointings and giftings. Churches will benefit the most as they open their doors to different ministries.

Others

The Word is going forth and we are doing our part. We have different jobs but the same purpose. Some go and some send so that the Gospel might be preached. Paul in his ministry was supported and prayed for by others. Others supported Jesus in His ministry. Even in the Old Testament, prophets and priests were dependent on others for physical help. Ministry is not something that can be accomplished alone. We need others. I am very conscious of my dependence on others in the Body of Christ. Others support our labor of love in the Lord. I am constantly amazed at the faithfulness and obedience of others. Gwen and I have learned to be independent of circumstances. We still need others. We have endeavored to trust the Lord for our livelihood yet we need others. It has not always been easy but we have experienced and learned a lot. We have learned that we are not alone. We have others. We have chosen to live by faith. We have given ourselves to ministry, to fasting and prayer. We have prayed and preached and prophesied. We have been busy in the Lord's vineyard. At times when supply has been underwhelming I have stood in faith trusting God. God used others to help. We have worked, prayed, fasted and did what our hand found to do. Fruit has been the result. What fruit? A fruitful relationship and fellowship with God and others is the result. I testify to the goodness and faithfulness of God for others and myself.

Our Battle

We are actually in a battle for the hearts of men. It takes a consorted effort to deliver those who are held captive by the devil in prisons of despair and doubt. Our job is to deliver living bread to dying men and women. The Body of Christ exists on this earth to set captives free, to destroy the works of the devil.

Our Father's Business

As prices increase it would be very easy to complain and grumble about the present economic situation. Fuel is increasing, food costs are soaring and many are feeling the pinch. This would put us in a precarious position ...but my God shall supply all your need according to his riches in glory by Christ Jesus. (Philippians 4:19). We are about our Father's business. This being the case, He pays the bills! We have a Heavenly Father who is the source of all our supply. He knows what we need before we need it and lavishes an abundance upon us. Every burden and every care he takes note of so that we can live without stress and without concern. To complain would in essence be saying that our Father is not great enough. To grumble is to say He is not concerned about our condition.

On the contrary, He is great enough and He cares affectionately and tenderly for each of us. He is ever attentive to our cries. In faith we acknowledge His abundant care and supply in our lives. We can rejoice and be thankful because we serve Him who is ever attentive to our needs. We are about our Father's business. A woman we prayed for was completely healed of cysts in her ovaries. One day they were there, the next day they were gone! The pastor called me and told me the young lady went to the doctor the day after our service and there was no trace of any growths or cysts. At another church, the pastor and I went out after the service and a man interrupted our conversation. As we sat and ate, right there in the restaurant the man received Jesus and was born again! We are about our Father's Business. Whether we are going with the message or sending the message by our prayers and financial support, we are about our Father's business and He will supply all our needs!

Our Joy And Reward

Paul said to Timothy, "And I thank Christ Jesus our Lord, who hath enabled me, for that he counted me faithful, putting me into the ministry;" (1 Timothy 1:12). Our reward lies not only in heaven or in the temporal blessings of this earth but in simply carrying out His will and knowing that our obedience brings blessing to many people. God counts us faithful putting us into ministry that brings joy, happiness and redemption blessings to precious souls. Along with heaven's reward and the temporal and physical blessings that God bestows on us, this is my joy and reward!

Our Own Company

As often as I can, I try to sit under other ministers in order to glean, learn, feed and receive a deposit of the Spirit of

God into my life and ministry. A mistake that ministers make is neglecting to feed on the Word. Every Believer ought to be a part of a local church or fellowship where they can be nurtured and fed. Being involved with a local church provides spiritual food and accountability with other Christians. If one is in the ministry leading a church or traveling, he has to make an extra effort to set aside time for fellowship, spiritual feeding and be accountable to other ministers of the Gospel on purpose! Many good men have fallen by the way side. They did not have those that they could confide in and who could speak into their lives. If you are in a position to do so, encourage your pastor to take time to sit and receive on occasion. It will be well worth it! In the New Testament we see that Jesus very often took time out to rest and receive. There is some indication in the Gospels that Jesus may have sat under the ministry of John the Baptist! We know this is so because he was familiar with his ministry and was baptized by John. Some even commented that Jesus was with John in the wilderness. And they came unto John, and said unto him, Rabbi, he that was with thee beyond Jordan, to whom thou barest witness, behold, the same baptizeth, and all men come to him. (John 3:26). How much time Jesus spent with John we do not know but He did spend time with John. We know that Jesus attended synagogue on a regular basis. Not only did he speak but we can also assume that He listened. It was the custom of the day to allow those who attended synagogue to speak or share from the written scriptures. Jesus apparently did so on a regular basis. And he came to Nazareth, where he had been brought up: and, as his custom was, he went into the synagogue on the sabbath day, and stood up for to read. (Luke 4:16). Jesus answered him, I spake openly to the world; I ever taught in the synagogue, and in the temple, whither the Jews always resort; and in secret have I said nothing. (John 18:20).

Jesus also took time aside from everyone just to spend time with His Heavenly Father in rest and prayer. And when he had sent the multitudes away, he went up into a mountain apart to pray: and when the evening was come, he was there alone. (Matthew 14:23). The practice of the early church was to be in continual fellowship and receive the Word. And they continued stedfastly in the apostles' doctrine and fellowship, and in breaking of bread, and in prayers. (Acts 2:42). The disciples had fellowship with their own. They had their own company. Every Christian needs a group that they can call their own. It is good and right to fellowship with the body of Christ at large but it is most important that we have our own company! This is where we go in time of trouble. This is where we go when we need to bare our hearts and share our burdens. This is the people to which we are accountable and we call on for ministry. It is our own company. And being let go, they went to their own company, and reported all that the chief priests and elders had said unto them. (Acts 4:23). Then pleased it the apostles and elders, with the whole church, to send chosen men of their own company to Antioch with Paul and Barnabas; namely, Judas surnamed Barsabas, and Silas, chief men among the brethren: (Acts 15:22). Make it your habit to be in fellowship with others. Make it a point to have your own company, i.e., your own church or fellowship group. Take time aside to feed on the Word and receive from others. Take time aside with your heavenly Father to rest and pray. It will enhance your walk with God and increase the fruit of your ministry. Together we walk in victory!

Our Wealthy Place

Thou hast caused men to ride over our heads; we went through fire and through water: but thou broughtest us out into a wealthy place. (Psalm 66:12). There is a place God wants to bring us to that is filled with His treasure. It is our wealthy place. If you have not discovered already, our Christian life is a journey. We are on a pilgrimage. Abraham was called out to search for a city which has foundations whose builder and maker is God. (Hebrews 11:10). And so we are called. We have ceased building our own lives and have allowed God to build in us his will and purpose. Thank God! The work that He has begun in us He will complete until the day of the Lord Jesus. (Philippians 1:6). God has brought us out so that He can bring us in to an abundant life and a new way of living. And he brought us out from thence, that he might bring us in, to give us the land which he sware unto our fathers. (Deuteronomy 6:23). We know that God has brought us out from sin and bondage but many of us have not come in to the new place, the wealthy place that He has prepared for us. Keep your eyes on the goal! He has not brought you out to leave you. He has brought you out to bring you in! God is not finished with you yet! Hold on to the promise of God! And let us not be weary in well doing: for in due season we shall reap, if we faint not. (Galatians 6:9).

Outward Thinkers

I want to be associated with outward thinking people. Outward thinkers are people who are not consumed with their own life, their own vocation and their own problems. I don't know how many times that I have spoken to someone and I have listened patiently as they explain all about themselves, their ministries, their experiences etc. etc. without even one question about my life, ministry or family. I am always overjoyed when someone asks about me and mine with genuine interest and concern. It is so rare that I have to mention it! One reason I am in the ministry is that I have a genuine interest in the welfare and well being of people. We all tend to be selfish at times. It is good to think of those who make our life better because they are in it. Remember your letter carrier, your garbage collector, your Sunday school teacher or your Pastor. Let them know that you are better because they are in your life! A hallmark scripture is "For God so loved the world that He gave........." (John 3:16). Our lives are changed forever because God loved us. He reached out to us and infused us with His life and presence. God gave to us! Life is all about loving and giving. Include others in your life. Stretch yourself to include others and give to others and love others. I want to think outwardly and bring joy and blessing to others. I am grateful for others including me in their life. I am thankful for those who think of me and remember me. Because I am included in the lives of others, I can include many others into my life.

A Part Of Everything We Do

Wherefore I also, after I heard of your faith in the Lord Jesus, and love unto all the saints, 16 Cease not to give thanks for you, making mention of you in my prayers; (Ephesians 1:15-16). God has raised up many as instruments of blessing to come alongside and help. We pray and give along with a multitude to spread the Gospel of Jesus Christ. A ministry trip to an Ohio church saw four people receive the baptism of the Holy Spirit. A week prior to that several were filled with the Spirit in South Carolina. Before that, I ministered in several churches where many were filled with the Spirit. Also, many were healed and touched by the power of God. The Word of God is going forth in power and setting captives free. I mention this; an instance in time, just a few meetings preaching the Gospel produces eternal fruit. I am aware that I am not alone. Those who pray and those who send are a part of everything I do. God is giving us fruit wherever we go and that fruit is the result of many who have come together to see it happen. I am only a small part of my own ministry! (It is because others are investing in the Gospel of Jesus Christ that there will be eternal benefits and fruit I receive abundance of help to preach, teach and travel from place to place to minister this powerful message from heaven. I am not alone. Working together we sow the seed of the Word of God and it is producing a mighty harvest. Paul wrote to the saints at Ephesus and told them that he thanked God for them and mentioned them in prayer. I am doing the same. Really, the epistles that Paul wrote to the churches were letters acknowledging their help and support of Paul and his ministry. Paul needed the support of churches and individuals in order that his ministry could continue. I am no different. We each have a part to play in taking this Gospel to hungry hearts. We are part of each other. We are partners together in the work of God.

Payday Is Coming

Praise God! The Gospel is the power of God unto salvation! Paul said that if we sow we shall reap IF we do not faint. Sometimes quitting seems easier than anything else but the truth is there is no reward in quitting. And let us not be weary in well doing: for in due season we shall reap, if we faint not. (Galatians 6:9) At times as I go I think, how can I go on? Weary and worn I ponder, Why not quit? But the fact is that there is no quitting for me. The alternative is too bleak. I can do nothing but fulfill the plan of God and trust Him that He will see me through. And in due season I will reap. Not my time but His time. Payday may not come every Thursday or at the end of the week. It may not come in two weeks or at the end of the month but one thing is for sure with God, PAYDAY IS COMING! He is faithful. He will see you through. You will make it with God. He loves us and He is watching over His Word to perform it!

Plan to Go, Plan To Give

The commission we have is to go and preach. The message we are preaching is Life to those who hear it. This Gospel message brings salvation, healing, wholeness, deliverance, peace, joy and prosperity. This message brings purpose for living and restores our fellowship with God and man. Jesus is our message. Jesus is our Life. Because of Jesus, we have purpose for our existence. I anticipate fulfilling His plan for my life. He is my Lord and Master! If there is one thing about our life in Christ it is that we no longer live for ourselves. We live with His purposes in mind. As we fellowship with Him, He imparts goals, vision, direction and purpose to our hearts. We no longer live for ourselves. We live for Jesus and for others. The life we live for others defines our success. His plans become our plans. His goals become our goals. I like what the Apostle Paul says in 2 Corinthians 9:6-7 concerning giving: "But this I say, He which soweth sparingly shall reap also sparingly; and he which soweth bountifully shall reap also bountifully. Every man according as he purposeth in his heart, so let him give; not grudgingly, or of necessity: for God loveth a cheerful giver." If we do not make it our purpose to give, if we do not plan to give, we will have very little effect on the Kingdom of God. As you endeavor to obey God with the money He entrusts you with, sit down and plan your giving. I plan to sow bountifully. I plan to give more and reach further than previous years. I plan to increase my Gospel reach.

Pleasing God

But to do good and to communicate forget not: for with such sacrifices God is well pleased. (Hebrews 13:16) I want to please Him on purpose, don't you?

Pray For Me

The Apostle Paul reveals much about prayer in his letter to the Ephesians. Praying always with all prayer and supplication in the Spirit, ... And for me, that utterance may be given unto me, that I may open my mouth boldly, to make known the mystery of the gospel, (Ephesians 6:18-19) To effectively communicate the Gospel, mysteries must be prayed out. Paul was able to preach boldly and with great results through prayers in the Spirit. The book of Acts is the account of a series of prayer meetings and their results. We have proven the axioms, "Only God can do the work of God," and "All the works of God are prayer works." "Anointed" ministry is clearly the result of intimacy with the Holy Spirit through prayer. James 5:16 declares, "...The effectual fervent prayer of a righteous man availeth much." The Amplified Version states it this way: "...The earnest (heartfelt, continued) prayer of a righteous man makes tremendous power available [dynamic in its working]."(AMP) As prayer goes to work, the power of God is released and the work of God is accomplished. I say along with the apostle Paul: Now I beseech you, brethren, for the Lord Jesus Christ's sake, and for the love of the Spirit, that ye strive together with me in your prayers to God for me; (Romans 15:30)

Prayer And Preaching

Prayer and the preaching of the Word are foundational to all Gospel ministries. Prayer prepares our heart and those to whom we are sent. Prayer goes into the heavens touching the heart of God. Preaching the Word touches the hearts of men. Marvelous things are accomplished when we pray. "Only God can do the work of God and He works through the prayer's of His people." Jesus was a man of prayer, a preacher of the Word, and a compassionate Healer. It is a stirring thought that we are temples of the Holy Ghost and God lives in us! God Himself is flowing through our hands and voices to bless and help people. We are His hands and His feet and His voice in the earth. I am thankful for the freedom and ability to share the Gospel of Christ.

Praying Out The Will Of God

There are many things we can involve ourselves in and many good works we can do but what counts is hearing His voice and being obedient. When eternity rolls around, it is not whether we accomplish much in the eyes of men but whether or not we heard His voice and pursued His plan for our lives. In what we refer to as the Lord's Prayer, Jesus includes, "Thy Kingdom come, thy will be done." (Matt 6:10) Our prayer is to enter into His will and do it. In the Garden of Gethsemane Jesus prayed, "Father, if thou be willing, remove this cup from me: nevertheless not my will, but thine, be done." (Luke 22:42) Our personal will and God's will are not always on the same page. This was true with Jesus and it is also true with us. Our flesh and fleshly mind will at times be contrary to God's purposes. Paul alludes to this in Romans chapter eight concerning a walk in the Spirit. Because the carnal mind is enmity against God: for it is not subject to the law of God, neither indeed can be. (Romans 8:7). We must choose the spiritual life. There are several Holy Spirit inspired prayers concerning knowing, walking and being established in the will of God. If it were not possible to miss God and miss His will for us it would not be necessary to pray these prayers. The will of God being fulfilled in our lives is not automatic. Being fruitful in our Christian lives is not automatic. We must pray out the will of God for our lives and then walk out the will of God. He will perform His will in our lives; Being confident of this very thing, that he which hath begun a good work in you will perform it until the day of Jesus Christ: (Philippians 1:6) but we must position ourselves to receive and walk in His will. First there must be a willing heart. Secondly, we must take a step of faith in His will. This step of faith begins with what Paul tells us. "Present your bodies a living sacrifice,",. (Romans 12:1) We take this first step of faith by presenting our bodies in prayer, worship, fellowship, meditation and study. Epaphras prayed fervently that the church at Colossae would stand perfect and complete in all the will of God. (Col 4:12). Earlier in this epistle Paul prays thus, "That ye might walk worthy of the Lord unto all pleasing, being fruitful in every good work, and increasing in the knowledge of God;" (Col 1:10). I often pray these and other Holy Spirit inspired prayers for myself and others. If we align ourselves with His will and purpose, He will perform what He has begun in us!

Praying Specifically

It is best for our prayers to be detailed and specific. Prayers like "I need a car" or "I need more money" are difficult for God to answer when we do not fill in the details. A car could mean a thirty-year old rust bucket held together with bailing wire. And if someone gives you a nickel you will have more money than you had before. Jesus explains how faith works in Mark 11:23: "For verily I say unto you, That whosoever shall say unto this mountain, Be thou removed, and be thou cast into the sea; and shall not doubt in his heart, but shall believe that those things which he saith shall come to pass; he shall have whatsoever he saith." We need to specifically spell out the details of what it is that we want from God. Think about it, yes. Dream about it, of course. But the most important thing is to say it out your mouth. Jesus does not stop here but continues by saying in Mark 11:24: "Therefore I say unto you, What things soever ye desire, when ye pray, believe that ye receive them, and ye shall have them." God works with our desires. He wants us to be specific and detailed when it comes to the things we desire. Begin to speak the specific desire of your heart. Say it and say it again. "Delight thyself also in the LORD; and he shall give thee the desires of thine heart." (Psalm 37:4). When our delight and words are of Him and about Him, He wants our desires to come to pass. Meditate, think and dream of Him. Ponder upon His Word. Speak His promise and your desire. It will surely come to pass!

Praying With All Prayer

Praying always with all prayer and supplication in the Spirit, And for me, that utterance may be given unto me, that I may open my mouth boldly, to make known the mystery of the gospel, (Ephesians 6: 18-19). Praying in the spirit is the making of my ministry. When I am asked, "What is God doing in your ministry?" My response is, "He is always doing marvelous things when I pray." If Jesus found it necessary to spend hours in prayer, how can God show up in my ministry without it?

Preach With Power

Through the years as we have ministered the Word in many situations, God has been good and faithful to confirm His Word and change lives by His power. The Gospel we preach is with power. Paul said it best, "And my speech and my preaching was not with enticing words of man's wisdom, but in demonstration of the Spirit and of power:" (1 Corinthians 2:4). Again in Paul's first letter to the Thessalonians: For our gospel came not unto you in word only, but also in power, and in the Holy Ghost, and in much assurance; as ye know what manner of men we were among you for your sake. (1 Thessalonians 1:5) The most noticeable difference in preaching is the power with which a message is delivered. It is that Truth that grips a heart with words that penetrate the innermost being of an individual and witness that the Words spoken are indeed the Truth. Luke, in his Gospel testified of the powerful preaching ministry of Jesus: And they were astonished at his doctrine: for his word was with power. (Luke 4:32). What produces this kind of preaching? There may be other ingredients but I want to list a few that I have understood to be components of my preaching and teaching ministry. 1. Have a real and true personal experience with God: Now when they saw the boldness of Peter and John, and perceived that they were unlearned and ignorant men, they marvelled; and they took knowledge of them, that they had been with Jesus. (Acts 4:13). And with great power gave the apostles witness of the resurrection of the Lord Jesus: and great grace was upon them all. (Acts 4:33). 2. A vibrant and consistent prayer life; And it came to pass in those days, that he went out into a mountain to pray, and continued all night in prayer to God. (Luke 6:12). But we will give ourselves continually to prayer, and to the ministry of the word. (Acts 6:4). Jesus and the apostles lived in prayer. This was their source of strength and effectiveness. The power of the church in the Book of Acts can be attributed to their prayers. The Book of Acts is really an account of the prayer life of the early church. 3. Faithfulness to study and understand how to use the Word of God in preaching, teaching and witnessing. And after certain days, when Felix came with his wife Drusilla, which was a Jewess, he sent for Paul, and heard him concerning the faith in Christ. 25 And as he reasoned of righteousness, temperance, and judgment to come, Felix trembled, and answered, Go thy way for this time; when I have a convenient season, I will call for thee. (Acts 24:24-25). Paul very skillfully preached with a good understanding of grace and law. The proper use of the Law of God and the Gospel is vital in bringing change to the hearts of men. The distinction between the Law and the Gospel is clearly taught in the Word of God. The combination of the condemning force of the Law and the saving comfort of the Gospel message to bring conviction of sin is the most powerful force in the conversion of sinners. To rightly divide the Word in this area is vital. Great Gospel preachers of old knew and understood the powerful use of the Law and the Gospel: "Before I can preach love, mercy and grace, I must preach sin, Law and judgment." John Wesley. "Conscience is the internal perception of God's Moral Law." Oswald Chambers. "The first duty of the gospel preacher is to declare God's Law and show the nature of sin." Martin Luther. "They will never accept grace until they tremble before a just and Holy Law." Charles Spurgeon. "Of this excellent use is the Law: it converts the soul, opens the eyes, prepares the way of the Lord in the desert, rends the rocks, levels the mountains, makes a people prepared for the Lord." Matthew Henry. A good understanding of how to handle law and grace in a sermon will make for powerful preaching. 4. A Vital and practical faith that expects results. And Stephen, full of faith and power, did great wonders and miracles among the people. (Acts 6:8). And what shall I more say? for the time would fail me to tell of Gedeon, and of Barak, and of Samson, and of Jephthae; of David also, and Samuel, and of the prophets: 33 Who through faith subdued kingdoms, wrought righteousness, obtained promises, stopped the mouths of lions, 34 Quenched the violence of fire, escaped the edge of the sword, out of weakness were made strong, waxed valiant in fight, turned to flight the armies of the aliens. (Hebrews 11:32-34). 5. A divine flow of compassion. And

Jesus, when he came out, saw much people, and was moved with compassion toward them, because they were as sheep not having a shepherd: and he began to teach them many things. (Mark 6:34). 6. Being filled and staying filled with the Holy Ghost. But ye shall receive power, after that the Holy Ghost is come upon you: and ye shall be witnesses unto me both in Jerusalem, and in all Judaea, and in Samaria, and unto the uttermost part of the earth. (Acts 1:8). And be not drunk with wine, wherein is excess; but be filled with the Spirit; 19 Speaking to yourselves in psalms and hymns and spiritual songs, singing and making melody in your heart to the Lord; (Eph 5:18-19). 7. The anointing that comes from staying in His presence: in the Word, worship and ministering to the Lord. The Spirit of the Lord is upon me, because he hath anointed me to preach the gospel to the poor; he hath sent me to heal the brokenhearted, to preach deliverance to the captives, and recovering of sight to the blind, to set at liberty them that are bruised, (Luke 4:18). Effectiveness and development in preaching the Word of God is an ongoing process for a powerful and fruitful ministry.

Prophecy, Dreams And Visions

The Holy Ghost administers God's purpose to us. Jesus is the Author and Finisher of our faith and He imparts to the Holy Spirit the plan and purpose for our lives. Howbeit when he, the Spirit of truth, is come, he will guide you into all truth: for he shall not speak of himself; but whatsoever he shall hear, that shall he speak: and he will shew you things to come. 14 He shall glorify me: for he shall receive of mine, and shall shew it unto you. (John 16:13-14). "He shall receive of mine, and shall shew it unto you." As we pray, worship and spend time worshipping the Father, things are happening. There is a communion of the Holy Spirit, Jesus and our human spirit.

Jesus imparts the plan of God for our lives into our spirits by communion with the Holy Ghost. Mysteries are unveiled to us and the Holy Ghost makes deposits into the hidden man of the heart. Prophecy, dreams and visions are the language of the Holy Spirit. These are the venues by which God imparts His plan and purpose for our lives. It is not your vision- it must be God's vision-- So many fail because they do not take time in His presence to get their vision from God. All ministry flows out of a relationship with the Holy Spirit: And it shall come to pass afterward, that I will pour out my spirit upon all flesh; and your sons and your daughters shall prophesy, your old men shall dream dreams, your young men shall see visions: 29 And also upon the servants and upon the handmaids in those days will I pour out my spirit. (Joel 2:28-29). and: And it shall come to pass in the last days, saith God, I will pour out of my Spirit upon all flesh: and your sons and your daughters shall prophesy, and your young men shall see visions, and your old men shall dream dreams: 18 And on my servants and on my handmaidens I will pour out in those days of my Spirit; and they shall prophesy: (Acts 2:17-18). These scriptures refer to the way the Holy Spirit communicates with us. The Holy Ghost is the agent by which prophecies, visions and dreams come and Jesus is the Originator and Author of the content. Prophecies, Visions and Dreams provide a foundation and purpose in life. They provide a picture of what we are to be and do. (When God communicates his directives via prophecy, vision or dream, it will last. It will stay with you. Visions and Dreams show us the final outcome. Prophecy provides a blueprint or a battle plan for our lives. They provide a glimpse into our future. Don't be overly concerned with how God will do it or when God will do it; just know that the vision is from Him and He will bring it to pass in His own time and in His own way. You do your part and God will do His part in bringing His plan to pass in your life. Prophecies (and prophecies of the scripture)., Visions and Dreams fuel everything you do. They ought to energize your every effort. There are two reasons for Vision; Firstly, They define your purpose for existence. Secondly, they keep you focused to direct and control all your activities. Your spirit man focused on the plan will eliminate every activity that does not contribute to seeing the dream come to pass. Visions not only show us the future but they also show us opportunities in our current circumstances. Jesus Christ is the Giver and Author of Prophecy, Visions and Dreams. You cannot succeed without them. They are the roadmap for a successful journey in God. Take time in His presence to receive God's plan for your life. He will fill your days with faith, hope and love as you enthusiastically pursue the dream He has given you.

Reaching Beyond

Let no man seek his own, but every man another's wealth. (1 Corinthians 10:24). Reaching out beyond your own need insures that the Gospel of Christ will be preached and your wants and desires will be fulfilled. It is God's desire to fulfill our desires when we deny ourselves and reach out beyond our own to touch those who cannot repay us. It is a life of faith. It is a walk of faith. But what an exciting way to live! When we release what is in our hand to God then He is obliged by His Word to release what is in His hand to us. When giving becomes a lifestyle things begin to change. We often do not know the how's, why's or when's of God's supply but He has never failed us. He is watching over His Word to perform it! Hallelujah!

The Reason We Give

Jesus had those who were close to Him that gave to Him and supported His earthly ministry: And it came to pass afterward, that he went throughout every city and village, preaching and shewing the glad tidings of the kingdom of God: and the twelve were with him, And certain women, which had been healed of evil spirits and infirmities, Mary called Magdalene, out of whom went seven devils, And Joanna the wife of Chuza Herod's steward, and Susanna, and many others, which ministered unto him of their substance. (Luke 8:1-3). These gave into Jesus' ministry because they loved Him. They had been delivered from their sin and bondage and they expressed their love by their gifts. This is the reason we give today. Because we love Jesus and He has saved us and set us free. How can we do anything less? You can give without loving but if you truly love you will be a giver.

The Reciprocal Action Of God

The Word of God tells us...for them that honour Me I will honour (1 Samuel 2:30). God has set in motion the law of reciprocity. Whatever you send out will come back with increase. Honor God and He will honor you.

Redeemed From The Curse

The Gospel is GOOD NEWS! I am continually in awe at the provision of God in Christ. We have been bought with a price. We are redeemed! Bought back and paid for by the death, burial and resurrection of Jesus Christ! In his letter to the Church at Galatia, Paul states clearly and succinctly the redemptive work of Jesus Christ: Christ hath redeemed us from the curse of the law, being made a curse for us: for it is written, Cursed is every one that hangeth on a tree: (Galatians 3:13). Redeemed from the curse of the law! Redeemed unto

God and redeemed from the curse! Today we are free from the curse of the law. The curse of the law includes poverty, sickness and spiritual death. God has provided everything we need to live a Godly, victorious life by Christ Jesus. We have been given the wonderful Name of Jesus. That one Name encompasses all of the redemptive names of Jehovah. The Name of Jesus, which is above every other name permits us to walk in the fullness of our redemption. The devil and demons are subject to that Name. Sickness has to bow to that Name. Poverty must flee at the mention of His Name! All that is in the Name belongs to us. Through His Name, God is present with us. He is our Righteousness and He is our Peace. He is our Shepherd and our Captain leading us in victory over our enemies. He is our Healer and our Provider watching over us to supply our every need. He is the Most High God. He is my Redeemer! The truth of our Redemption is unveiled. Religion offers nothing but the pure and simple gospel message will put you over in life. I am thankful for the revelation of His Word. I am thankful for this GOOD NEWS Gospel!

Redeeming The Time

Verses in the Book of James ring true as life carries on. .....For what is your life? It is even a vapour, that appeareth for a little time, and then vanisheth away. (James 4:14). As the years go by I realize more and more how short our time is on this earth. More and more I want every waking moment to count for Jesus. Time is so very precious! I believe that when we live each moment for Jesus, those moments lived for Him can never be lost but go on for eternity. What we do with our time, our talents and our money can never be lost if we use them for the Gospel of Christ. I am a positive person but I know that we live in a wicked world. There are many things that pull us in so many directions. Many of these things are needful and beneficial. Yet with so many demands on us, we must "buy back" our time for Jesus. What do I mean by buy back? I mean where days and moments have been stolen or misused we must take each moment available to us and make these moments count for Jesus. This is what Paul meant when he stated in Ephesians: Redeeming the time, because the days are evil. (Ephesians 5:16). Moses looked back at his life knowing full well that he needed to make the best of his time serving the Lord. He had spent 40 years in the world, 40 years on the backside of the desert and now he had 40 years remaining to serve the Lord. Moses was 80 when he began to really live for God in a fruitful way. Moses is a good example of redeeming time! No matter how late it seems we can begin again. We can have a fresh start with renewed dedication and consecration serving God! So teach us to number our days, that we may apply our hearts unto wisdom. (Psalm 90:12).

Returning Thanks

I know that people are grateful to God for all that they receive but it sure is nice when someone acknowledges their blessing in a tangible way. Jesus experienced this when He healed ten lepers. They went away rejoicing but only one returned to give thanks to the one who brought deliverance to him. And as he entered into a certain village, there met him ten men that were lepers, which stood afar off: 13 And they lifted up their voices, and said, Jesus, Master, have mercy on us. 14 And when he saw them, he said unto them, Go show yourselves unto the priests. And it came to pass, that, as they went, they were cleansed. 15 And one of them, when he saw that he was healed, turned back, and with a loud voice glorified God, 16 And fell down on his face at his feet, giving him thanks: and he was a Samaritan. 17 And Jesus answering said, Were there not ten cleansed? but where are the nine? 18

There are not found that returned to give glory to God, save this stranger. 19 And he said unto him, Arise, go thy way: thy faith hath made thee whole. (Luke 17:12-19). I am resolved to be like this Samaritan. I want to be like the one who returned to glorify God and acknowledge His blessing. The result is that this man was not only cleansed, he was made whole! We have seen countless lives changed and touch by the anointing and the Word of God. Whether or not we have helped anyone, it is God who helps us all and giving to God's work on the earth acknowledges His blessing. I am always grateful for those who return thanks in a tangible way. I want to be one who returns thanks. I will return to glorify God.

The Rewarder

At times it seems we do much for what seems to be very little in return. Payday may not come when we think it ought or in the manner we deem fit but payday is coming! Again I say God is faithful. An older minister friend of mine, a mentor in my life, shared with me that God always gives an honest day's pay for an honest day's work. I have seen this truth over and over again in my life. When I am obedient to do what God has called me to do He is always faithful to provide in abundance. I know that as you obey Him He will supply all that you need. For God is not unrighteous to forget your work and labour of love, which ye have shewed toward his name, in that ye have ministered to the saints, and do minister. (Hebrews 6:10). Also, I want to say again that it pays to serve the Lord. Payday does not always come every Friday nor does it come regularly at the end of every month but there is no question that payday will come with God! His blessing is yours! This is a faithful saying, and these things I will that thou affirm constantly, that they which have believed in God might be careful to maintain good works. These things are good and profitable unto men. (Titus 3:8). Godliness is not found in a pious look but it is found in good works. Your godly works will bring reward because He is THE REWARDER of those who are diligent. God rewards consistency and faithfulness. For bodily exercise profiteth little: but godliness is profitable unto all things, having promise of the life that now is, and of that which is to come. (1 Timothy 4:8). God will see to it that you are rewarded because He is THE REWARDER and He is FAITHFUL!

Run Your Course With Joy

Not long after graduating from Bible School, I began working for Rex Humbard Ministries in Akron, Ohio. I was twenty years of age and throughout my adult life, I have not pursued anything other than ministry. I have done many things with ministry in mind. Whatever I have had to do in order to fulfill my ministry. I have bagged groceries, pumped gas, stocked shelves, painted houses, delivered office supplies, worked as a bricklayer's helper and for the U.S. Census. I have done all these things and more, the whole while pursuing the ministry. A steady flame has burned within me to preach this glorious Gospel. Gwen and I have gone through different seasons in our lives and we have encountered countless obstacles and challenges in the ministry God has given us. We have both determined that in spite of anything and everything we will do our best to follow God and minister to people with God's ability. It seems at times that setbacks and disappointment have ruled the day but I will gladly suffer any thing thrown my way in order to fulfill the divine and holy call. I say with the Apostle Paul, "None of these things move me!" I have determined to finish my course with joy! But none of these things move me, neither count I my life dear unto myself, so that I might finish my course with joy, and the ministry, which I have received of the Lord Jesus, to testify the gospel of the grace of God. (Acts 20:24). I run my race with joy in the Holy Ghost and testify to the Gospel of the grace of God.

A Sacrifice Pleasing To God

Paul spoke of sacrificial giving in his letter to the Philippians' Church. The Church at Philippi was the only church that remembered him while he was held prisoner in Rome. Now ye Philippians know also, that in the beginning of the gospel, when I departed from Macedonia, no church communicated with me as concerning giving and receiving, but ye only. 16 For even in Thessalonica ye sent once and again unto my necessity. 17 Not because I desire a gift: but I desire fruit that may abound to your account. 18 But I have all, and abound: I am full, having received of Epaphroditus the things which were sent from you, an odour of a sweet smell, a sacrifice acceptable, well pleasing to God. 19 But my God shall supply all your need according to his riches in glory by Christ Jesus. 20 Now unto God and our Father be glory forever and ever. Amen. (Philippians 4:15-20). It seems many times that it is the minority that meets the need. Paul declares that because of their faithfulness in supporting him that God would undoubtedly supply all their need but more than that, their sacrifice was received and well pleasing to God. He receives your offering as a sweet smelling sacrifice offered up before God. This is what Paul declares the offering from the Philippians' Church sent by Epaphroditus to be. Paul goes on to say that because of their sacrifice, God Himself would supply all their need. Not only does God receive your gift as an act of adoration and worship toward Him but He also considers it a seed planted that will bring forth a harvest for the one who gives. Beyond that there is a spiritual harvest of righteous fruit for the Kingdom of God that remains forever! (As it is written, He hath dispersed abroad; he hath given to the poor: his righteousness remaineth for ever. Now he that ministereth seed to the sower both minister bread for your food, and multiply your seed sown, and increase the fruits of your righteousness;) (2 Corinthians 9:9-10).

Satan is a Defeated Foe!

As I have travelled and preached through the years, God has been gracious to grant fruit for our labors. Many have been touched by the power of God, born again, filled with the Holy Ghost, healed and ministered to in various ways. On one particular occasion a woman who was deaf was healed in one of our meetings and several others received notable miracles. By the Holy Ghost and the gifts of the Spirit I have spoken into many lives and the Word of the Lord brought healing and blessing. In another instance, a man came into my meeting and reported that eight years prior he had come into one of our tent meetings and was gloriously saved. He told me that all these years later he is still in church serving the Lord along with his wife and seven children. Glory to Jesus! Another man came up to me and introduced me to his 14-year old daughter. He reminded me that years ago I had prayed for him and his wife to conceive and then spoke the Word of the Lord that they would have a daughter who would be born and grow up loving Jesus. Praise God forevermore! I mention these things because even while good things are happening, the devil never ceases to stir up trouble. I think even more so as we do damage to his kingdom. I have come to an understanding that if good things are happening the devil is close by attempting to stir up trouble. Nevertheless, Satan is a defeated foe! As we march forward, we continue to fight the good fight of faith and exercise our victory over the enemy!

When bad things begin to happen that are seemingly unprovoked and come out of nowhere, I know that we are a threat to the enemy and we are causing no small stir among the legions of hell. The battle rages and we must enforce Satan's defeat. I have learned to laugh at the devil! We cannot be defeated and we will not quit! The devil is a liar! We have encountered supernatural opposition over the years while pursuing the call of God on our lives. At times it seems the attacks are stepped up a notch or two. I believe it is because we are a legitimate threat to the devil. You want to know what I say about it? So what! He cannot stop us or defeat us! Just another mountain to be cast into the sea! I laugh and rejoice because we win! Ha, Ha, Ha devil! The following scriptures explain the devil's demise. In them we are assured that Jesus defeated Satan long ago and his future is set. And he said unto them, I beheld Satan as lightning fall from heaven. (Luke 10:18). And the devil that deceived them was cast into the lake of fire and brimstone, where the beast and the false prophet are, and shall be tormented day and night for ever and ever. (Revelation 20:10). Thank God, we win!

Sealed With The Knowledge Of His Coming

The message of the soon return of Jesus is extremely important because many are not ready! The message of His soon return is a catalyst in the Church to prepare the Bride for the Bridegroom. Our message is Jesus is coming soon! Our end time doctrine can be summed up in two words: BE READY! Lift up your eyes and look. Jesus is coming soon. Now is the time to watch for His soon coming. Watch therefore, for ye know neither the day nor the hour wherein the Son of man cometh. (Matthew 25:13). I love this quote from Maria Woodworth Etter concerning her special call to preach, " ... To give the Household of Faith their Meat in due season; to give the last call to the Gentile sinners, the last Call to the Marriage Supper of the Lamb, for His wife is about to enter the marriage relationship; and to get those who have been called to be established, to be faithful and true, that they may be anointed with the Holy Ghost and with power, and sealed with proper knowledge of His coming." Wow! Sealed with the knowledge of His coming. This is our call. This is our purpose. Jesus is coming soon! Watch! Pray! Be Ready! Jesus is coming back in like manner as He was taken up! Maranatha!

The Seed Is The Word

Now the parable is this: The seed is the word of God. (Luke 8:11). Only eternity will tell the results of seeds planted. From our vantage point it is impossible to accurately measure the impact that teaching, preaching and the ministry of the Spirit have on those who embrace it. In New Jersey a couple from a Dutch Reformed Church visited one of our services and was filled with the Holy Ghost. I trust in the Word of God to do its job. Most of the time I never hear the results of my ministry. On occasion I am privileged to receive feedback and get testimonies of the impact the Word has had. Attitudes are changed, heart repentance, yieldedness to God's purposes, so many results that come from the Word of God being preached. The Word preached is a seed sown. I have heard sometimes eight or ten years later of the effect that our ministry has had on an individual or a church. I remind myself of the power and potential that is in a seed. Know that the seeds you plant are bringing forth amazing results. You may not always see it now but the fruit of your seeds sown will be known when eternity rolls around. We continue planting and believing in the seed. We continue to go forth sowing the good seed of the Word of God. The result? For the earth bringeth forth fruit of herself; first the blade, then the ear, after that the full corn in the ear. (Mark 4:28).

Seed Sowers

The sower soweth the word. (Mark 4:14). I preach, teach and distribute the Word of God here and around the world. I have been privileged to reap great harvests through the years with many saved, healed and filled with the Holy Ghost. A multitude of lives have been touched and changed as a result of preaching this glorious Gospel. Regardless of the results in any particular meeting, one thing has been consistent throughout many years of ministry. That is the consistent sowing of the Word of God. There have been many occasions where I thought absolutely nothing was accomplished when, to my surprise, years later I heard of a life being changed because a gospel seed took root and produced fruit. I thank God for the outcome and good reports that have been brought to my attention concerning our ministry. Abundance of fruit has accompanied the preaching of the Word of God. As admirable as these results are, I am reminded that the most important thing is that we are continually and consistently sowing the seed of the Word wherever we go. I lay no claims to amazing results or any results for that matter. I have no ability to bring about salvations, healings and miracles. When it seems that fruit is not forthcoming or seemingly very little takes place in a meeting, I remember that it is the Word of God sown in the hearts of men and women that is important. Our purpose is not to Christianize the world but to evangelize the world. We are seed sowers. I cannot save anyone, heal anyone or produce a miracle. The Father Himself has the power to save. My job is to sow the seed and simply trust God to do the rest. When we do our part then God can do His part. And they went forth, and preached every where, the Lord working with them, and confirming the word with signs following. Amen. (Mark 16:20). My part is to preach and teach. I leave the results in His hands. When I am faithful to preach His Word, God is faithful to confirm His Word.

Seedtime And Harvest

Spring is a Blessing! I always enjoy springtime. It seems the earth is waking again from a long winter's nap. Trees start to blossom, flowers are blooming and gardeners are at it again planting seeds. One thing the Lord promised us is that as long as the earth remains, there will be seedtime and harvest. Because of the wickedness upon the earth, God destroyed all of mankind with a flood. Only Noah and his family survived. After the devastation God looked upon the earth and said that He would never judge the whole earth in this manner and He gave us a promise: And the LORD smelled a sweet savour; and the LORD said in his heart, I will not again curse the ground any more for man's sake; for the imagination of man's heart is evil from his youth; neither will I again smite any more every thing living, as I have done. 22 While the earth remaineth, seedtime and harvest, and cold and heat, and summer and winter, and day and night shall not cease. (Genesis 8:21-22). God's promise is that as long as we are on the earth, seedtime and harvest will work. That's a promise! It works in nature and it works concerning spiritual things. We sow and we reap and we reap what we sow! Seedtime and harvest allow us to take this Gospel around the world. We are sowing good seed that will surely reap a harvest. This is the law and promise that God Himself has set in motion. Once you plant the seed, God is watching over His Word to perform it. (See Jeremiah 1:12). We can be sure that when we continually plant the seed of the Word of God, we will continually experience a harvest.

Shout Grace!

When we find ourselves facing problems, obstacles and trouble that we cannot handle, we need to take action. There are things that we face in life that are clearly overwhelming. It is good to be aware of our human condition. When we become aware of our own limits we may then wholly lean on His everlasting arms. I think one reason God cannot undertake and move on our behalf is because we have too much confidence in our own ability. The Word of the Lord came to Zerubbabel stating just that: Then he answered and spake unto me, saying, This is the word of the LORD unto Zerubbabel, saying, Not by might, nor by power, but by my spirit, saith the LORD of hosts. (Zechariah 4:6). Our help comes from the Lord. Our own efforts are futile in the face of the world, the flesh and the devil. Don't forget all the benefits of the Lord. We have grace for every situation and circumstance. This is why Zechariah goes on in verse 7: Who art thou, O great mountain? before Zerubbabel thou shalt become a plain: and he shall bring forth the headstone thereof with shoutings, crying, Grace, grace unto it. (Zechariah 4:7). It is not your ability that will get you through, it is the grace of God. Grace is God's free gift to you. It is His ability and power. Grace is God's Riches At Christ's Expense. Grace is God's unmerited favor to us. We cannot work for it and we do not deserve it. When a mountainous problem faces your life, speak to that mountain! Shout to that mountain! Shout GRACE! GRACE! GRACE! You have just unleashed the ability and power of God into you situation. Open your mouth and shout GRACE! What is this grace? It is Christ's work of redemption wrought for us! Think about this scripture: He that spared not his own Son, but delivered him up for us all, how shall he not with him also freely give us all things?

(Romans 8:32). All things are ours through Jesus Christ! We are blessed and we have His grace bestowed upon us. Not only have we received His grace but also God gives more grace. Thank God for His grace! It belongs to us through Jesus Christ! Shout grace to your body! You are healed! Shout grace to your finances! He is your provider! Shout grace to your marriage, to your ministry, to every area of your life. We have His grace!

Simple Faith In A Simple Message

I do not ever want to take for granted the truth that we preach. The simple message of a new life in Christ is changing the world one person at a time! It is a simple faith in the death, burial and resurrection of Jesus Christ that saves. Religion, good works or morality never saved anyone. It is Jesus, up close and personal. He is my Savior; He is my Healer; He is my Provider; He is my Shepherd; He is my Righteousness; He is my Peace; He is my Joy; He is my Redeemer; He is my Friend; He is my Lord and King. I am in Christ. You are in Christ. Together we make up the Body of Christ in this world. We have the answer to the world's problems. In Christ, we are the answer to the world's problems. It is no more complicated than this. Jesus is coming soon.

Simple Plan Of Preaching

The plan of salvation is so simple! All that is required of us is to hear and believe! I say with the apostle Paul; "For I am not ashamed of the gospel of Christ: for it is the power of God unto salvation to every one that believeth; to the Jew first, and also to the Greek." (Romans 1:16). What a thrill to know that the knowledge of this gospel releases power to save! Power to heal! Power to deliver! Power to change lives!

When this gospel is preached and believed it works in amazing ways. Again, Paul tells the Thessalonians that faith makes the difference; "For this cause also thank we God without ceasing, because, when ye received the word of God which ye heard of us, ye received it not as the word of men, but as it is in truth, the word of God, which effectually worketh also in you that believe." (1 Thessalonians 2:13). Our job is not to change the message. We do not have to extrapolate it, take away from it or add to it. It is powerful just as it is. Our job is to share it. Give it away. Send it away. Get it to people who are hungry and needy. We are a delivery service, distributing Living Bread to dying men. "For whosoever shall call upon the name of the Lord shall be saved. How then shall they call on him in whom they have not believed? and how shall they believe in him of whom they have not heard? and how shall they hear without a preacher? And how shall they preach, except they be sent? as it is written, How beautiful are the feet of them that preach the gospel of peace, and bring glad tidings of good things!" (Rom 10:13-15).

Smack Dab In The Middle Of God's Perfect Will

Our desire is to be in the right place at the right time, smack dab in the middle of God's perfect will. Only by prayer and the Holy Ghost can we do this. We do not always know the details of our future but we do know Him who has the future in His hand! But as it is written, Eye hath not seen, nor ear heard, neither have entered into the heart of man, the things which God hath prepared for them that love him. But God hath revealed them unto us by his Spirit: for the Spirit searcheth all things, yea, the deep things of God. (1 Corinthians 2:9-10). As we pray, God reveals His will by the Holy Ghost. If we do not pray we will not know His plan and purpose. Along with a working knowledge of His Word, (His

Word is His will), prayer is vital to knowing and fulfilling the will and purpose of God for our lives. Paul prays this way in Colossians 1:9-10, "For this cause we also, since the day we heard it, do not cease to pray for you, and to desire that ye might be filled with the knowledge of his will in all wisdom and spiritual understanding; That ye might walk worthy of the Lord unto all pleasing, being fruitful in every good work, and increasing in the knowledge of God;". Again, Paul mentions the prayers of Epaphras in Colossians 4:12: "Epaphras, who is one of you, a servant of Christ, saluteth you, always labouring fervently for you in prayers, that ye may stand perfect and complete in all the will of God." In Hebrews 13:21 we read: "Make you perfect in every good work to do his will, working in you that which is wellpleasing in his sight, through Jesus Christ; to whom be glory for ever and ever. Amen." Pray for and desire His will and you will surely find it!

Sowing God's Word Into Your Heart

Always be conscious of the law of sowing and reaping. The principle of seedtime and harvest is interwoven into the fabric of our lives and ministries. Because sowing and reaping, is a spiritual law, it will work whether we want it to or not. This law is always in operation so we should make it work to our advantage. There are two things to keep in mind concerning the law of seedtime and harvest. First, you always reap what you sow and secondly, you will always reap more than you sow. Since we know this to be true, we can determine the kind of harvest we will receive because we know what we have planted. If we want to prosper and have good success in our lives we should be ever conscious of this law and apply it each and every day. We should apply it when it comes to our giving and receiving but more importantly we should apply it when it comes to the seed of God's Word sown in our hearts. The Word sown in our hearts will determine our health, our wealth, our wisdom and our blessings from God. Our actions will be determined by the abundance of faith and the Word of God in our hearts. Giving and being a blessing is not limited to what we have in our pockets but our giving AND receiving is limited to what we have in our hearts. This is the reason we build the Word of God into our lives because it will determine our actions and our blessings. This is why Joshua said that meditation is the key to prosperity and success in every area of our life: This book of the law shall not depart out of thy mouth; but thou shalt meditate therein day and night, that thou mayest observe to do according to all that is written therein: for then thou shalt make thy way prosperous, and then thou shalt have good success. (Joshua 1:8). Paul stated in his letter to the Corinthians that God will give seed to the Sower. You see that this scripture reveals our giving is not limited to what is in our bankbooks but what is in our hearts: And God is able to make all grace abound toward you; that ye, always having all sufficiency in all things, may abound to every good work: (As it is written, He hath dispersed abroad; he hath given to the poor: his righteousness remaineth for ever. Now he that ministereth seed to the sower both minister bread for your food, and multiply your seed sown, and increase the fruits of your righteousness;) Being enriched in every thing to all bountifulness, which causeth through us thanksgiving to God. For the administration of this service not only supplieth the want of the saints, but is abundant also by many thanksgivings unto God; (2 Corinthians 9:8-12). Take time to confess God's promise in regards to financial blessing. The time you spend sowing God's Word in your heart is not lost time. It will produce a harvest for you. The following are a few scripture seeds for finances that you can "sow" into your heart. Scripture Seeds For Finance (Plant these scriptures in your heart for a financial harvest) Deuteronomy 8:18- But thou shalt remember the LORD thy God: for it is he that giveth thee power to get wealth, that he may establish his covenant which he sware unto thy fathers, as it is this day. Ecclesiastes 5:18-19- Behold that which I have seen: it is good and comely for one to eat and to drink, and to enjoy the good of all his labour that he taketh under the sun all the days of his life, which God giveth him: for it is his portion. Every man also to whom God hath given riches and wealth, and hath given him power to eat thereof, and to take his portion, and to rejoice in his labour; this is the gift of God. Job 22:24- Then shalt thou lay up gold as dust, and the gold of Ophir as the stones of the brooks. (*Note-Dust returns on a daily basis and the stones in a brook are without number. No matter how much you clean, there will be more dust the next day and no matter how many stones you take from a brook you can never remove them all) Job 36:11- If they obey and serve him, they shall spend their days in prosperity, and their years in pleasures. Psalm 23:1- The LORD is my shepherd; I shall not want. Psalm 35:27- Let them shout for joy, and be glad, that favour my righteous cause: yea, let them say continually, Let the LORD be magnified, which hath pleasure in the prosperity of his servant. Psalm 66:12- Thou hast caused men to ride over our heads; we went through fire and through water: but thou broughtest us out into a wealthy place. Psalm 112:3- Wealth and riches shall be in his house: and his righteousness endureth for ever. Proverbs 13:22- A good man leaveth an inheritance to his children's children: and the wealth of the sinner is laid up for the just. Proverbs 19:17- He that hath pity upon the poor lendeth unto the LORD; and that which he hath given will he pay him again. 2 Corinthians 8:9- For ye know the grace of our Lord Jesus Christ, that, though he was rich, yet for your sakes he became poor, that ye through his poverty might be rich. Make these scriptures personal, read them over and over again. Plant them deep in your heart! They will produce a harvest for you!

Speak Good Things

There is protection, blessing and help in Words. Words and prayers surround us and affect us in a powerful way. The Book of Proverbs tells us that words produce life or death: Death and life are in the power of the tongue: and they that love it shall eat the fruit thereof (Proverbs 18:21). Words can bubble over with faith or be filled with doubt. I am aware of words. Faith-filled words are vital to a victorious walk. When you pray, speak words of life over yourself, your family and loved ones. Pray and speak these words over your life: "I am blessed and grace abounds toward me. I have life, health and strength for my family and myself. I am safe in the secret place. I will not be afraid. Money comes to me. I have an overflowing abundance of wealth and plenty to give into the Kingdom of God and to others. I enjoy great favor with God and man and many effective doors are open to me to preach the Gospel. Grace and favor are increasing in my life. Spiritual wisdom and revelation are increasing and I am fruitful in every good work. The supply of the Spirit is increasing in me. I have plenty of help to accomplish all that God has called me to do. The Spirit of God leads me continually and my steps are ordered of the Lord. I am filled with love, joy and peace in life and ministry. I am blessed and happy in Jesus' Name!" Speak good things over your life. Make your prayers and words work on your behalf.

Special Providence For The Righteous

God is good and He provides for all living creatures. The scriptures tell us: Who giveth food to all flesh: for his mercy endureth for ever. (Psalm 136:25). He causeth the grass to grow for the cattle, and herb for the service of man: that he may bring forth food out of the earth; (Psalm 104:14). Behold the fowls of the air: for they sow not, neither do they reap, nor gather into barns; yet your heavenly Father feedeth them. Are ye not much better than they? (Matt 6:26). God also provides for the wicked as well as the righteous: That ye may be the children of your Father which is in heaven: for he maketh his sun to rise on the evil and on the good, and sendeth rain on the just and on the unjust. (Matt 5:45). Our Heavenly Father is so generous He provides for all living things. Not only does He care for the righteous but He also cares and provides for sinners! God's provision extends to all of creation but the scriptures tell us that as His very own children we can expect special favor and treatment. You really are God's favorite! God is the source of all that we need and desire. Knowing that He is our provider we live for Him and honor Him. We can expect special intervention in our lives in the way of protection and provision. When we as God's children respond to His love, He lavishes abundant blessings upon us. God is involved in the minute details of our lives. There is special providence exercised by God on behalf of the righteous. Obey Him, do the right thing and His hand will rest on you mightily. The steps of a good man are ordered by the LORD: and he delighteth in his way. (Psalm 37:23). But seek ye first the kingdom of God, and his righteousness; and all these things shall be added unto you. (Matt 6:33). For those who will yield to His plan and will there is great benefit. Continue to submit yourself under His mighty hand. For he that will love life, and see good days, let him refrain his tongue from evil, and his lips that they speak no guile: 11 Let him eschew evil, and do good; let him seek peace, and ensue it. 12 For the eyes of the Lord are over the righteous, and his ears are open unto their prayers: but the face of the Lord is against them that do evil. (1 Peter 3:10-12). How simple it is to have a good life!

Spiritual Fathers

Several years ago I attended the funeral service of Dr. Kenneth E. Hagin. This precious man of God was a father in the faith to me. I am grateful for having known him and to have graduated from his Bible School. There are few ministers in my life that have had the impact that "Dad" Hagin had on me. Paul tells us we have many teachers but not many fathers. Just as we honor and respect our parents in the flesh, we ought to honor those who are fathers of spiritual things in our lives. For though ye have ten thousand instructors in Christ, yet have ye not many fathers: for in Christ Jesus I have begotten you through the gospel. (1 Corinthians 4:15). What is a spiritual father? Paul was an apostle but that does not necessarily make him a spiritual father. A spiritual father may be one who led you to Christ but it is much more than that. A spiritual father is one who has nurtured you in the Gospel. He is one who has strengthened and helped you to grow in God. A spiritual father is not just a teacher of spiritual things but is an example of how to walk and live in Christ. I have been with men who are great preachers and teachers and have had mighty ministries but I would not necessarily want to follow the example they set. A spiritual father is someone we are to emulate and imitate. Thank God there are those who have been strong and faithful too! Dad Hagin was a man of faith but he was also a man of great love. All who were close to him never knew him to say anything derogatory about anyone ever! A spiritual father is someone we choose to have a continual influence over our lives. Many pastors are spiritual fathers to many in their churches but that does not make them a spiritual father to everyone in their church. Some in the church act like spiritual orphans. They do not receive their pastor as a "Pastor" and they have no spiritual father. Your pastor may or may not be a spiritual father in your life. It is important that we have and receive a spiritual father. A Spiritual Father is someone who has begotten you in Christ or nurtured you in the Gospel. They have not only instructed you but they have been an example of Christian life and character to you. A spiritual father is one whom you may follow and emulate. A spiritual father has the right to speak correction into your life and has a continued influence upon your life. I thank God for the "fathers" in my life.

Spiritual Practice

In Matthew's Gospel, Jesus mentions three fundamental spiritual practices in His Sermon on the Mount. They are: giving, praying and fasting. These are keys of the Kingdom that we are to utilize in this life. Each of these spiritual or (if I can use the word in a good sense), religious practices carries with them their own reward. There is a reward from God for giving. There is a reward from God for praying. There is a reward from God for fasting. There certainly are other spiritual and religious practices that are beneficial and carry their own reward but these three are fundamental spiritual keys that are universally understood. Every culture and every world religion understands and implements these spiritual keys. Many thousands and millions worship false Gods and others vainly worship the True and Living God. But if any will seek God with all their heart He will be found of them and He will reward them. Giving, praying and fasting are means by which an individual can seek God with all his heart. And ye shall seek me, and find me, when ye shall search for me with all your heart. 14 And I will be found of you, saith the LORD: ......(Jeremiah 29:13-14). In Acts chapter ten we see the door of the Gospel was opened to the gentile world because of the spiritual practices of one, Cornelius. When Cornelius began to seek God, He was not a Christian and had never experienced the new birth. He was not even Jewish! However, he loved the Jewish nation and was most likely a Jewish proselyte familiar with the Old Testament scriptures. Cornelius was giving, praying and fasting in His search for God and meaning in life. Luke, the writer of the Book of Acts records that God was moved by the spiritual exercise of Cornelius. The Angel tells Cornelius that his prayers and giving had ascended to the throne of God. And he said unto him, Thy prayers and thine alms are come up for a memorial before God. (Acts 10:4). Because of the actions of Cornelius, he and his entire household were saved and filled with the Holy Ghost. Up until this time the Gospel had only been preached among the Jews but now we see an open door for the Gospel to the gentiles. The giving, prayers and fasting of Cornelius opened the door for the Gospel to be preached to the entire gentile world. God is the Rewarder of them that diligently seek Him. Continue your spiritual practice of giving, praying and fasting. He will reward you!

Stewardship Principle

I believe God wants to entrust much to those who are faithful. There is the principle in the scripture concerning sowing and reaping and seedtime and harvest. This law says that you will reap what you sow and you will always reap more than you sow. We ought to apply this principle for good in our lives in every area including our finances. There is another rule in scripture that goes beyond mere sowing and reaping. I refer to the stewardship principle. This principle states that if I am faithful with little, the Lord will entrust me with much. Along with blessing comes authority and responsibility. You cannot increase in authority without increasing your responsibility. God is looking for those individuals with whom He can entrust and make them stewards over much. He is looking for those who are faithful with what they have so that He can use them to finance the Gospel around the world. He is looking for those who will be responsible and faithful to the task at hand. This goes far beyond sowing and reaping. By committing to stewardship we become agents by which God can direct funds to spread the Gospel throughout the earth. I believe God wants to entrust thousands and millions to individuals to take the Gospel to the ends of the earth. We are not just planting seed in the ground expecting a harvest. As faithful stewards, we become partners with God in spreading the Gospel! Moreover it is required in stewards, that a man be found faithful. (1 Corinthians 4:2). And he said unto him, Well, thou good servant: because thou hast been faithful in a very little, have thou authority over ten cities. (Luke 19:17). You will reap what you sow for an abundant harvest but more than that you are a steward of the Gospel of Christ. Your giving assures that the Gospel continues to march forward in the earth.

Striving Together In Prayer

As a preacher, It is a privilege for me to share the Word of God and minister the Spirit! I cannot do this alone. Partners and friends help me preach the Gospel. They pray for me and I pray for them. I continually ask that God's highest and best be established in their lives. I pray the prayers of Epaphras: Epaphras, who is one of you, a servant of Christ, saluteth you, always labouring fervently for you in prayers, that ye may stand perfect and complete in all the will of God. (Colossians 4:12). I pray the Spirit inspired prayers found in Ephesians chapters one and three and Colossians Chapter one.

I do not take my responsibility to pray lightly. Praying for others is an important part of my day. Paul's letters were primarily written to those to whom he had taken the Gospel. He continued to pray for them and minister to them and in return they were praying for Paul and supporting his ministry. This interaction is vital to the success of any ministry. We believe in God and we must believe in each other in the Body of Christ. Now I beseech you, brethren, for the Lord Jesus Christ's sake, and for the love of the Spirit, that ye strive together with me in your prayers to God for me; (Romans 15:30).

Strong Churches

Through the years we have endeavored to bring a greater understanding to churches in regards to the move of the Spirit in churches. We have done so by demonstrating and flowing in the gifts ourselves and also offering teaching and training in the gifts of the Spirit especially the operation of tongues and interpretation during the worship service. Years ago Kenneth Hagin Senior was often asked, "What is the Lord doing in our day?" His reply was that, "God is raising up strong churches walking in the Word and moving in the Spirit." I believe that is what God continues to do. He is raising up strong Word and Holy Ghost Churches. I often refer to a portion of Kenneth Hagin's prophecy from 2003 where he stated, "....Make your church not only a Word Church but a Holy Ghost Church." There is a great need for local churches to learn to flow and move in the Spirit. The gifts of the Spirit must be allowed to operate freely respecting the order that Paul laid out in 1 Corinthians chapter fourteen. Much of this chapter has been overlooked and misunderstood. Because of this, I have focused much of my ministry along these lines. Developing Strong Word and Spirit Churches is the order of the day. People are desirous of a genuine move of the Holy Spirit in their churches. We are seeing much excitement and enthusiasm for this subject matter. I am glad to be teaching and preaching these truths concerning the move of the Spirit in the local church. This is a message whose time has come.

Supply Is In His Name

The Lord is our Shepherd, Jehovah Ra-ah and we do not want for any good thing. He is Jehovah-Jireh, He sees ahead, prepares for us and supplies our every need. Not only that but He is El Shaddai! The God who is more than enough! Praise God! Supply is in His Name! He has everything you need.

Take Time To Give Thanks

I have learned over the years to take time to count my blessings and thank God for all the good things He has bestowed upon me. We serve a great God and a wonderful Savior. We have much for which to be thankful.

Take Time To Pray

Prayer is vital to all that we do and accomplish. Without regular prayer it is impossible to stay in tune with the plan of God. I thank God for His written Word but it must be approached with prayer. It is prayer that keeps us balanced in our thinking and in our doctrine.... especially prayer in the spirit or in tongues. Paul tells us in Romans 8:14, "For as many as are led by the Spirit of God, they are the sons of God." This is speaking of a mature walk with God. Much is revealed to us in the scriptures concerning the general will of God for our lives. We know to do certain things because it is spelled out for us in the scriptures. Even applying the revealed will of

God requires much prayer. Jesus told His disciples in the garden of Gethsemane to pray with Him so that they would not enter into temptation: And he cometh unto the disciples, and findeth them asleep, and saith unto Peter, What, could ye not watch with me one hour? Watch and pray, that ye enter not into temptation: the spirit indeed is willing, but the flesh is weak. (Matthew 26:40-41). It requires prayer to walk in what is clearly seen in the scriptures. How much more must we pray to receive guidance concerning things that are not specifically written in the pages of the Bible? There are so many choices and so many decisions to make in life. It can become overwhelming. This is why prayer is so necessary, especially praying in the spirit or praying in tongues. We should pray long enough so that our mind gets quiet and settled and peace pervades our entire being. As we practice this kind of prayer on a consistent basis we will begin to know what to do and what not to do simply by following peace in our hearts. We may spend more or less time in prayer on any given situation or event in our lives but when we pray through to peace we will have our answer from heaven. If we are to navigate successfully in life we must pray. Praying in the spirit will quiet our minds so that we can hear God deep down in our hearts. To walk in the Spirit we must apply the revealed will of God then follow peace in our hearts. Take time to pray in order that you may walk in the success and victory that belongs to every child of God. Be careful for nothing; but in every thing by prayer and supplication with thanksgiving let your requests be made known unto God. And the peace of God, which passeth all understanding, shall keep your hearts and minds through Christ Jesus. (Philippians 4:6-7).

Tangible And Intangible Fruit

Now he that ministereth seed to the sower both minister bread for your food, and multiply your seed sown, and increase the fruits of your righteousness;) (2 Corinthians 9:10). Bread for food and fruits of righteousness: God gives to us things tangible and things intangible. There are things money can buy and things money cannot buy. He supplies our needs and gives us the desires of our heart. These are things tangible. He also gives us His love, joy, peace, and spiritual blessings. These are things intangible. The fruit of righteousness is what we produce from doing right and living right in His presence. Our life consists of loving God and loving others. We exist to bless others and demonstrate real Christianity to the world.

Tangible Presence

There is a way to experience God's presence wherever we are. As Believers in Christ we all enjoy His indwelling presence. God indwells every genuine Christian. The earth is filled with His omnipresence. The beauty of God's creation reveals His eternal power and Godhead. Even sinners can enjoy this aspect of His presence though they may not acknowledge or recognize it. The presence I am speaking of is His tangible presence. This is a presence that can be felt. It is a presence that invades the physical realm. This particular aspect of the presence of God can accompany us and increase in our lives. I believe that in these last days, God's tangible presence will be experienced on the street and in the market place. More and more congregations are moving into a greater depth of worship. There is quite a stir amidst denominational folks toward a "Presence Centered" worship. There is a way into the presence of God and a way to bring God's presence upon us. That way is worship. As more and more Christians emphasize spiritual worship there will be the tangible presence of God manifest in their midst. As more Christians experience the presence of God in their services there will be a greater manifestation of the glory of God. We all need times of rest and refreshing and worship is the key to entering the tangible presence of the Lord over in the realm of glory. The Father seeks those who are indwelt by Him to worship Him. His power and presence come to those who worship. As Believers enter into private times of worship, they will carry His Presence into their daily lives. Power and presence are not just relegated to the church sanctuary. As Believers enter into worship on a daily basis, His power and presence will be manifest wherever they are. Repent ye therefore, and be converted, that your sins may be blotted out, when the times of refreshing shall come from the presence of the Lord; (Acts 3:19). Be a worshipper. There is no higher manifestation of faith and no greater act of love toward God than the simplicity of worship. Spend your days in worship and you will spend your time in His presence. Continue in His presence and you will continually be revived and refreshed. Be strengthened and blessed in His Presence over in the realm of glory.

Teach Us To Number Our Days

Time is of the utmost importance. The Apostle Paul reminds us in Ephesians 5:16 that we must redeem our time. Each of us has only so much time to let our light shine on this earth. Time is our greatest and most precious resource. First, we must put a priority on our time. There are so many things to do and the important things will not get done if we do not prioritize our time. Jesus said it this way, But seek ye first the kingdom of God, and his righteousness; and all these things shall be added unto you. (Matthew 6:33). Start every day doing first things first. Start every day seeking

God with prayer, Bible study and worship. The second thing is that time is limited here on this earth. We need to serve the Lord with the understanding that we only have so much time to work with. There will come the day when our time on this earth will run out. With this in mind we should make every day count for Jesus. Moses prayed this prayer, So teach us to number our days, that we may apply our hearts unto wisdom. (Psalm 90:12). The third thing about time is that it goes by so swiftly. As a child, time seemed to go by so slowly. Now it seems the last few years have gone by with lightning fast speed. Life goes by very quickly. For us who are living in the last days, time has been shortened. Things are speeding up. Jesus is coming soon. Make your days count for Jesus. It won't be long and eternity will roll around and time will no longer be what it once was. James looks realistically at life when he said: Whereas ye know not what shall be on the morrow. For what is your life? It is even a vapour, that appeareth for a little time, and then vanisheth away. (James 4:14). Let each moment you live count for Jesus.

Thanksgiving

Surely the righteous shall give thanks unto thy name: the upright shall dwell in thy presence. (Psalm 140:13). America is a great nation! Imagine a day set-aside just to give thanks! The men who came up with this day in America were great and godly men and they made America great and godly. I believe that America is still great and godly because it is made up of people who continue to acknowledge God in their lives and continue to give thanks. Those who acknowledge God and give thanks enrich my life. I am blessed because others are thankful. The world is blessed and made better by people who acknowledge God and are thankful. I say with the

Apostle Paul: We give thanks to God and the Father of our Lord Jesus Christ, praying always for you, (Colossians 1:3).

They Loved Not Their Lives

...**a**nd they loved not their lives unto the death. (Revelation 12:11). Greater love hath no man than this, that a man lay down his life for his friends. (John 15:13). The above Scriptures speak of selfless acts of love done for others. There is something about the love of God that gives itself away and offers itself up regardless of the consequences. Acts of bravery and acts of courage throughout history have stood out and shined forth among men because we find an element of this high kind of selfless love in these actions. Desmond Doss received the highest award for valor in action during World War II. He was the only noncombatant to receive the Medal of Honor. He was a Christian Seventh-day Adventist and conscientious objector. He refused to carry a weapon while carrying out his duties as a medic. He served on the island of Okinawa and under heavy fire by Japanese snipers he safely lowered over 75 wounded soldiers from atop a cliff. He recalls that the bullets were as thick as bees flying around his head yet not one bullet struck his body. Desmond never carried a gun or fired a shot. With no regard for his own personal welfare, one by one Desmond lowered the wounded men to safety. This is an exceptional example of one who lay his life down for his friends. Alvin C. York, a Christian, was drafted into the Army from the mountains of Tennessee during World War I. He was conflicted in his heart concerning the 6th commandment, "Thou shall not kill." Still he wanted to serve his country. The Army was going to allow him a religious exemption but he decided to stay and serve his country. York mused in his diary; he was no longer worried about his own safety on the battlefield or about his own soul.

He was concerned about what a Christian soldier should be concerned about: for those who passed out into the deep of an unknown world and left no testimony as to the welfare of their souls. In Europe, in the Argonne Forest, on a given day, he and his company were pinned down by sniper fire from three machine gun nests. He and seven others were pinned down by rapid machine gun fire while the rest of his company lay dead or wounded. In a battle that was his alone, Alvin York single handedly took out 35 machine guns, killed 24 Germans and took 132 enemy soldiers captive that day. Alvin was promoted to the rank of Sergeant and was presented the Medal of Honor. Later, when ask about the conflict in his soul concerning the killing of men, he said that he knew if he had not taken out those machine gun nests that many more men would have died that day. Sergeant York is another shining figure of one who loved not his life unto death. Joan of Arc was visited by an angel and called by God as a teenage girl to lead the armies of France. England and France had been at war for nearly 100 years when Joan came on the scene. She led the French into battle after battle and won great victories for France. This young girl's selfless act stirred a nation and rallied its armies to victory. For all her efforts she was tried by the church as a heretic and burned at the stake. Not long after her death the war between France and England ended. She was an amazing young lady called by God to end this conflict that raged for 100 years. Today, she is regarded by the Catholic Church as a saint. The list goes on throughout human history of the men and women who loved not their lives unto the death. Each had such love for their fellow man that they lay down their own lives for their friends. Our greatest example of course is Jesus Christ Himself. He went to the cross, bore your sin and mine, went to hell and suffered the torments of the damned. For three days and nights, Jesus remained in the heart of the earth satisfying the claims of Divine justice for the world's sin. Greater love hath no man than this! Because of His great sacrifice there have been a multitude of smaller sacrifices by men and women full of the love of God on behalf of mankind. This is the love of God that gives itself for others. This love lays its life down with no regard for itself. The Holy Ghost sheds this same love abroad in our hearts. I want to live my life so that others may benefit. I want my life to count for others, don't you? The love of God is impacting lives. Only God has the power to change a life but he works through your sacrifice and mine. He works through your gift and mine.

They Will Be Saved

If someone will send a Preacher, the Gospel is preached and people will hear. If people hear, they can believe the Word. If they will believe it they can act on the Word. If they act on the Word it will transform their lives; i.e. they will be saved! The Sender's gift sets God's purpose in motion. Revival comes by the preaching of the Word. One small act of obedience sets in motion God's purpose...It is awe inspiring to think of it. I am thankful for those Senders sending me to preach the Gospel. Senders sow in order that the seed of the Word of God might be planted. There is no telling what will be the result of the Word planted in a person's heart. A natural seed is sown and a Spiritual harvest is the result. A financial seed will produce an untold spiritual harvest.

This Gospel Shall Be Preached

And this gospel of the kingdom shall be preached in all the world for a witness unto all nations; and then shall the end come. (Matthew 24:14). I preached my first sermon in 1977 at the age of seventeen. Since then I have preached an inestimable number of times anywhere I have had the liberty.

I know that I will be preaching a host of sermons yet to come, travel thousands of miles to do so and share the love of God wherever I go. It is vital to God that this Gospel is preached. A primitive tribe of Indians in South America heard the message of Jesus' death, burial and resurrection. When they realized Jesus was their substitute for sin they shouted, danced and celebrated for over two and a half hours! What power is in this Gospel! I am humbled to think of the privilege I have to preach this Glorious Good News. When you see the Gospel have its affect on people to inspire and change their lives you are never the same. When the revelation of the Gospel's affect and power comes, you would do anything, give anything and make any sacrifice necessary to see it preached and demonstrate its power. Paul the Apostle wrote, for I am not ashamed of the gospel of Christ: for it is the power of God unto salvation to every one that believeth; to the Jew first, and also to the Greek. (Romans 1:16). I also say, I am not ashamed because the Gospel given to me and the Gospel that I preach has the power to save and heal and set captives free! I have given myself for the preaching of this Glorious Good News! I have offered my life as a witness and testimony of its power! I carry this Glorious message to hurting and hungry people. Labor in the Lord's vineyard. Deliver the power of God to those who otherwise would not hear it. Do your part. Make a difference. This is God's richest and best! And this gospel of the kingdom shall be preached in all the world for a witness unto all nations; and then shall the end come. (Matthew 24:14).

Thrilled With This Gospel

I am always thrilled that this Gospel we preach continues to meet needs and satisfy hearts. I have said often with the Apostle Paul, "I am not ashamed of the Gospel of Christ!"

Why Paul? Because it is the power of God unto salvation to everyone that clings to it, that adheres to it and that believes it! This Gospel will change lives! It will change hearts! It will heal bodies! It will bring peace where there is no peace! It will produce joy where there is nothing but sorrow! This Gospel is the power of God to all who will believe it and receive it! This Gospel gives us a hope and a future! This Gospel delivers the captive and opens blinded eyes! This is the Gospel of God! It is my Gospel. It is our Gospel. It is the only Gospel that will suffice for a sin sick, disease ridden world. I can sense it. There is healing in these words. Why? The Gospel of Jesus Christ is being proclaimed. Let your heart be stirred with His goodness. My heart is stirred. He not only proclaims His goodness to us, He wants to astound and stagger us with His glory. He wants to overwhelm you with His love! My prayer is that you will be a copious receiver of His love. I pray that you are a partaker of His extravagant goodness!

Together We Go

And how shall they preach, except they be sent? as it is written, How beautiful are the feet of them that preach the gospel of peace, and bring glad tidings of good things! (Romans 10:15). We are going with the Gospel of Christ. I mean to say that TOGETHER we are going with the Gospel of Christ. Alone we do nothing. Together we go with this glorious Gospel. We have a full schedule going with the Gospel. The plan and vision of God ahead of us is to go with the Gospel. Churches, tents, auditoriums, open air, wherever... we are going and we are preaching. Whoever believes our Gospel... their lives are changed. They are saved, healed and delivered. They are moved and they are stirred to move in close to God. They are filled with the knowledge of

His will. They receive understanding and wisdom because we are going and we are preaching this glorious Gospel.

Together We Win!

We are the Body of Christ and whatever we accomplish, we accomplish together. Paul tells us in 1 Corinthians 12:18-20, "But now hath God set the members every one of them in the body, as it hath pleased him. And if they were all one member, where were the body? But now are they many members, yet but one body." There is a story told in the Old Testament when Aaron and Hur held up the arms of Moses during a battle against Amelak. The Lord spoke to Moses to hold up his hands during the battle. As long as Moses had his hands in the air the battle went well. But when he put his hands down the children of Israel began to lose the battle. Aaron and Hur stepped-up and held up the hands of Moses. Glory to God! With the help of Aaron and Hur the battle was won! Then came Amalek, and fought with Israel in Rephidim. 9 And Moses said unto Joshua, Choose us out men, and go out, fight with Amalek: to morrow I will stand on the top of the hill with the rod of God in mine hand. 10 So Joshua did as Moses had said to him, and fought with Amalek: and Moses, Aaron, and Hur went up to the top of the hill. 11 And it came to pass, when Moses held up his hand, that Israel prevailed: and when he let down his hand, Amalek prevailed. 12 But Moses' hands were heavy; and they took a stone, and put it under him, and he sat thereon; and Aaron and Hur stayed up his hands, the one on the one side, and the other on the other side; and his hands were steady until the going down of the sun. 13 And Joshua discomfited Amalek and his people with the edge of the sword. (Exodus 17:8-13). We are fighting the good fight of faith. It is a fight that we win but we cannot fight alone. In a very real sense we are in a battle for souls. The lives of men and women, boys and girls hang in the balance. The Word we are preaching is the key that will win hearts and set captives free. Even as Aaron and Hur supported Moses in the battle, we must support each other. Together we win! We are the Body of Christ. We are laborers together in Christ. We are fellow soldiers in the greatest battle of our lives.

Tossing Tracts

Traveling, teaching, preaching and ministering the uncompromised Word of God! Lives are transformed, Churches are revived and God's Word is glorified. Christ is our strength to take this Gospel to the world. I pray that we stand perfect and complete in all the will of God and that we are unhindered to take this Glorious Gospel to the uttermost parts of the earth. Everyone must have an opportunity to hear the Gospel. Many throughout the world have never even heard the Name of Jesus. We need to pray and take the Word to them. If we do not, who will? A friend of mine was on a train in India and he was prompted to toss gospel tracts out the open door of the train. After he returned home he received a letter from a stranger in India. While plowing a field an Indian man noticed a piece of paper stuck in a tree. He sent his son to retrieve the fluttering piece of paper. The boy climbed the tree and returned the paper to his father. It turned out to be one of the tracts my friend had thrown from the train! Upon reading the tract he gave his heart to the Lord and went back to his village to share what he had found. It turned out that years before, missionaries had come to this little village but the people pushed them out and treated them very badly. Since that time the village had experienced trouble and difficulty continually. After reading the tract, the people felt this was a sign from God that He was giving them another chance. The entire village repented of their sin, believed the

Gospel and was gloriously saved! This is the power of the Gospel we preach! I am taking this Gospel to a world desperately in need. There is no other message like it. Everybody deserves a chance to hear it for the first time. Many have never heard it for the first time.

The Two Way Street

"If we have sown unto you spiritual things, is it a great thing if we shall reap your carnal things?" (1 Corinthians 9:11). It is a two way street.

The Ultimate Gift

Christmas is an awesome time of year! Christmas time is a time for giving and receiving. There is an excitement around our house as we prepare for Christmas day. With our four daughters we have had a busy time, looking for just the right gifts to put under our Christmas tree. As parents I think it is just as exciting for Gwen and I to see our girls open their presents as it is for them to receive them. It has taken extra time, extra work and extra money to give our girls their hearts desire for Christmas but their excitement and joy has been worth it all. I know when our Heavenly Father sent His only Begotten Son into this world He must have felt a similar thrill to know that the people who had been separated from Him by sin would receive the greatest gift He could offer. He thought about this gift very carefully. The Father was giving His best and greatest that we might have redemption through the gift of His Son. He gave so that we might experience the love, joy and peace of Heaven. It was the ultimate gift. I cannot describe it any better than what John said in his Gospel, "For God so loved the world, that he gave his only begotten Son, that whosoever believeth in him should not perish, but have everlasting life." (John 3:16). The Bible explains that one may give all they have and not have love. Genuine love on the other hand will always give. The essence of love gives itself away. God gave us His only Son, Jesus. The Gospel demonstrates ultimate love; the Gospel unveils supreme sacrifice and the greatest gift ever given. This love was manifest so that we might enjoy a life in Christ and the Father might have a family.

Variety Of Ministry

There is so much need in the churches for variety of ministry. People receive differently from different gifts. A pastor cannot accomplish what an evangelist can in the church and vice versa. An evangelist cannot do for the people what a pastor can do. When we rightly discern the Body of Christ we will be a healthy church. In order to rightly discern the Body of Christ we must recognize the need for different ministries in the church. I am well aware of my inadequacies in ministry. On the other hand, other well-equipped ministers of the Gospel cannot do what I can do with the gift God has given me. Together we move ahead and accomplish all God has for us.

A Very Present Help

We must have a sufficient supply of the Holy Ghost in our lives. Praying for one another is so necessary! The prayers of others will provide a supply of the Spirit! We all need the prayers of family, church and friends in the Body of Christ. These prayers make a difference! Paul, writing from prison, mentions this in his epistle to the Philippians. For I know that this shall turn to my salvation through your prayer, and the supply of the Spirit of Jesus Christ, (Philippians 1:19). Paul coveted the prayers of the Philippians' Church because he knew that their prayers supplied a deposit of the Spirit of God that he needed to survive his ordeal. The Church at Philippi prayed for Paul and supported him financially. You are not alone in the Church of the Lord Jesus! We are members of the same family. The Family of God! Do not isolate yourself. We are members of His Church! He is a very present help in time of trouble. Reach out for help. It is readily available!

We Are Not Saved

The harvest is past, the summer is ended, and we are not saved. (Jeremiah 8:20). These are quite possibly the saddest words in scripture. We only have a limited time to bring in the harvest. Millions are waiting to hear. There are sheaves to be gathered. The harvest must be brought in. Before the harvest is past, before the summer ends, they must hear. When they do, they will be saved.

We Are One Another

When we go we go we do not go alone. When we preach we do not preach alone. His Spirit joins us together. We do not function separately. We function together! We are not one-alone, we are one another! How many times the scriptures mention one another! John 15:12- This is my commandment, That ye love one another, as I have loved you. Romans 12:10- Be kindly affectioned one to another with brotherly love; in honour preferring one another; Romans 15:7- Wherefore receive ye one another, as Christ also received us to the glory of God. Romans 15:14-....admonish one another. Galatians 5:13-...by love serve one another. Colossians 3:16-... teaching and admonishing one another in psalms and hymns and spiritual songs, 1 Thessalonians 5:11- ...edify one another, even as also ye do. Hebrews 3:13- But exhort one another daily, while it is called To day; James 5:16- Confess your faults one to another, and pray one for another, that ye may be healed. We need each other. Don't ever isolate yourself! We are to function as many members but one Body of Christ. I am keenly aware of the need to flow with others. God's blessing is on unity. Behold, how good and how pleasant it is for brethren to dwell together in unity! (Psalm 133:1).

We Are The Body Of Christ

We are a Body, the Body of Christ. We work together, flow together and we are all needed to accomplish God's purpose. Paul was so eloquent in 1 Corinthians twelve in describing the Body of Christ: For our comely parts have no need: but God hath tempered the body together, having given more abundant honour to that part which lacked: 25 That there should be no schism in the body; but that the members should have the same care one for another. 26 And whether one member suffer, all the members suffer with it; or one member be honoured, all the members rejoice with it. 27 Now ye are the body of Christ, and members in particular. (1 Corinthians 12:24-27). As a member of the Body of Christ, I am grateful for my fellow members. I am able to do what I do because of other members in the Body. You are able to do what you do because of other members in the Body. We are the Body of Christ fulfilling His plan and purpose in the earth. I cannot do it without you. You cannot do it without me. In Christ we work together and carry out His will. I am with you and you are with me and so we are altogether as we march along.

We Have The Message

We have seen the Lord move mightily in our meetings. People have been saved, healed and filled with the Holy Spirit. We have freely given to many ministries and outreaches in order to further the Gospel of Christ. I believe in this

Gospel! It delivers results! Blind eyes are opened and deaf ears unstopped! A notable miracle took place under our tent when a blind lady received her sight. In Baltimore, a young lady's deaf ear is opened. In Romania, a five-year-old child born blind was healed. In Bulgaria, after rubbing spittle in a woman's eyes she saw perfectly after two decades of blindness. In India 230 precious souls received Jesus as Lord and Savior. A man who had been paralyzed and could move neither arms nor legs was completely healed. A mute girl was healed who had never spoken. After the dumb spirit was cast out she spoke for the very first time in her life. Backs have been healed, the barren have given birth, legs have grown out, cancer has left and growths have disappeared. The Word of God has worked mightily! We have years of traveling across this nation and other nations. My entire adult life I have preached. I preached my first sermon in 1977 at the age of 17. The Lord willing, I will preach until Jesus comes. Wherever, whenever, however... I will preach this Gospel to the ends of the earth. We have faced many obstacles and we continue to preach. We are not discouraged. Why? We have the message that will transform the world. All must hear. All must know. We have the answer to the world's problems.

We Must Continue To Preach

Our heart is to share Jesus with a troubled world. To bring liberty to those who are bound. Each one of us has a ministry whether or not we do it as a vocation or just as a Christian letting our light shine. Wherever we go and whomever we meet gives us the excuse to share Jesus. On one occasion, my family and I spent two days visiting New York City, Ellis Island and the Statue of Liberty. As we were waiting on the ferry to take us to Liberty Island where Lady Liberty stands, a woman sat down beside my wife and me. In our conversation we discovered that she was from northern India and by her dress and makeup I knew she was a Hindu. Certain parts of Northern India are less than 1% Christian. It is made up mostly of Hindus and Muslims with a few Buddhists and other religions scattered throughout. I gave her a gospel tract entitled "Who Is Jesus". She gratefully received it and kissed the pamphlet and began to read. I am sure she had heard of Jesus but most likely knew very little about Him. By believing what was written on the tract her life would be transformed. Many believe that there is no significant difference between Christianity and other world religions. People think as long as they believe in God and are sincere they will be all right. In New York City a man told me he did not believe in organized religion. His religion was a private belief in his heart. The problem with having your own private religion is you are susceptible to any and every lie the devil has floating in the air. If having their own beliefs can save people, Jesus need not have died on the cross. If being morally good can save people then the sacrifice of Christ was for nothing. If you can be saved by any other religion of the world, then there is no need to share the Gospel of Jesus Christ. Missionaries, evangelists and preachers are wasting their time if there is another way to be saved. The devil is a liar and he has filled the earth with his lies and false religions. This is the very reason we must open our mouths and declare The Truth of God's Word. While the religions of the world require obedience to rules and creeds, Christianity is unique among them all because it is based upon a relationship with the person of Jesus Christ, who is God. Christianity is unique because salvation is by grace alone. No one merits or earns salvation. It is the free gift of God. Christianity is unlike any religion in the world. Every world religion is based on the merits of what people do. They all contend it is good works and morals that save. The problem with a man-based religion is that he can never produce a righteousness that will satisfy the Holy God of Creation. Only Christianity, among all the religions of the world says there is nothing that we can do to save ourselves. We can only believe what Jesus has done for us in His death, burial and resurrection. What a revolutionary thought. Man cannot save himself. He can only trust God to do what he could never do. One True God revealed through Jesus Christ, God's only Son. We can be saved by no other name under heaven. For whosoever shall call upon the name of the Lord shall be saved. (Romans 10:13). None of the world religions claim a personal relationship with God, only Christianity. They all believe one must do something in order to earn salvation. None believe that Jesus is God. So you see we must continue to preach, persuade, convince and reason for the Truth of God's Word. I continue to preach this Gospel.

We Need Each Other

Very little can be accomplished by ourselves but when we flow together and focus on a common goal, with God, nothing is impossible to us. Our goal is reaching the world with this simple Gospel message. We all need help to fulfill the vision God has placed in our hearts. 1 Corinthians 12:20-25 is so real to me: "But now are they many members, yet but one body. 21 And the eye cannot say unto the hand, I have no need of thee: nor again the head to the feet, I have no need of you. 22 Nay, much more those members of the body, which seem to be more feeble, are necessary: 23 And those members of the body, which we think to be less honourable, upon these we bestow more abundant honour; and our uncomely parts have more abundant comeliness. 24 For our comely parts have no need: but God hath tempered the body together, having given more abundant honour to that part which lacked: 25

That there should be no schism in the body; but that the members should have the same care one for another." To say it simply, I need you. You need me. We need each other.

We Preach Not Ourselves

For we preach not ourselves, but Christ Jesus the Lord; and ourselves your servants for Jesus' sake. (2 Corinthians 4:5). The ministry of giving and prayer validates the ministry of teaching and preaching! The one thing does not get done without the other. I cannot exist and fulfill my call without those who give and pray. It is difficult to express my gratitude towards God for the obedience and faithful ministry of those who take it upon themselves to help me in the cause of Christ. I am humbled and honored by the faith of others to pray and send me to preach. As Paul declared, "I am your servant for Jesus' sake!" I am a Gospel messenger sharing Good News because someone is sending me. I have this message of Gospel Truth burning in my heart. At times, the frustration I feel because I cannot reach further with this glorious Gospel message.... Well, there are those who are easing my burden and granting me joy in my efforts to take this Gospel to all who will hear. I am enabled to go through open doors as they are afforded me. I am thankful for those who believe in this Gospel message. I can go because someone believes in the work of teaching, preaching, praying and ministering this glorious Gospel of Christ.

Weeping First

He that goeth forth and weepeth, bearing precious seed, shall doubtless come again with rejoicing, bringing his sheaves with him. (Psalm 126:6). First there must be passion. A desire to see the lost saved, the sick healed and the empty filled. Pray. Pray, Pray, Pray. Passion and desire prepares the way to fruit.

What Brings Revival?

Several years ago while in Detroit, Michigan, I was wonderfully surprised when one my 'heroes' in the faith walked into the meeting I was conducting. I had never met him prior to this occasion. "Holy Hubert" Lindsay had been preaching for over 60 years all over the United States and in over 60 different nations of the world. He owned a tent bigger than Oral Robert's tent, he preached open-air meetings and crusades all over the world and preached in many volatile situations during the turmoil of 1960's and 70's on university and college campuses. He was the original campus preacher and some regard him as the Father of the Jesus people movement of the 1960's. He preached under a tent in Tupelo, Mississippi in the spring of 1936 just prior to that horrible tornado that wiped out a huge portion of the city and left more than 100 people dead within the city limits. Elvis Presley's grandmother brought Elvis to the meetings in her arms. Her life and home were spared in the tornado. Hubert preached during the Watt's riots, the aftermath of the Kent State shootings and during the student demonstrations on California's USC and Berkeley Campuses. Ronald Reagan, who was the Governor of California at the time, told Brother Lindsay that he had saved the California taxpayers millions of dollars in crowd control expenses during the student uprisings of the 1960's. Brother Hubert would interrupt the student gatherings and begin preaching the Gospel. They often forgot what they were demonstrating about and directed their attention toward "Holy" Hubert. He saw many come to Christ as a direct result of his preaching. After the service he asked me a pointed question. "What brings revival?" I responded,

"Prayer." He said no. I spoke again, "A sovereign outpouring." Again he spoke with a resounding no. I asked him, "Brother Lindsay, what brings revival?" He said to me, "The one thing that will bring revival is the preaching of the Word of God." I spent the next day with him talking about the Word of God. We talked about numerous subjects through the day. As we spoke, a recurring theme arose in our conversation. Again and again he said, "Preach Jesus and Him crucified." I have determined to stay away from doctrinal disputes, hobbyhorses and peculiar interpretations of scripture. I will preach the Word in simplicity and power. This is the one thing that will stir up revival in the land. I have no greater task before me than to pray and preach the Gospel.

What Is God Doing?

Where we are received, we see miracles. People are saved, healed and filled with the Holy Spirit. The anointing brings results. It may wax or wane but it is that brushed on, painted on, power and ability of God that makes the difference. Instant miracles, pain leaving, arthritis healed, growths disappearing all are the result of the presence of the Holy Spirit and the anointing. The anointing produces testimonies of cancers being healed, salvations, rededications and reconsecrated lives to Christ. On one occasion a woman came to church for the first time in her life when we were ministering and gave her heart to Jesus. She was in her mid twenties and had never been inside a church her entire life. It is not uncommon in our ministry to see any where from two to twenty individuals come forward to receive the Baptism in the Holy Ghost. I never get tired of seeing people filled with the Spirit. It is thrilling to think of the potential for ministry that is in each person after they are filled with the Spirit. The gifts of the Spirit are moving in such a beautiful way. We continue to encourage churches and pastors to make room and give time for a move of the Spirit in their services. Many are experiencing a fresh move of the Holy Spirit in their churches. I believe this is the tip of the iceberg concerning what God wants to do with His people. People ask, "What is God doing in these last days?" He is building strong, Holy Ghost Churches! He is building strong people and strong churches that know how to cooperate with the Holy Ghost. He is raising up men and women obedient to His Spirit. He is raising up churches moving in the anointing of God. In 1987 I was in the home of a missionary to the Navajo Indians out in the western part of the United States. As I lay upon my bed, the Holy Spirit spoke to my heart a scripture... Zechariah 8:9; Thus saith the LORD of hosts; Let your hands be strong, ye that hear in these days these words by the mouth of the prophets, which were in the day that the foundation of the house of the LORD of hosts was laid, that the temple might be built. As I read the scripture the Lord whispered to my spirit, "Son, I want you to go and strengthen the hands of Believers in order that they may get about the work of the ministry that my Temple might be built in the earth." We continue to preach and teach the uncompromising Word of Faith to all who will listen and receive. This Gospel must be preached in the power and demonstration of the Holy Ghost. Jesus is coming soon!

Whatsoever Thy Hand Findeth To Do, Do It

Over the years as I have sought the will of God it wasn't always clear what I was to do but like Joseph, I have taken care of the business at hand and God has blessed. I find that many people who are looking for God's guidance and plan do not consider what is before them. They are always praying and wondering what does God want them to do but they don't DO anything. God has opportunities for us as close as the nose on our face but He expects us to get busy. Begin to DO what you know to do. God will bless your efforts and His will becomes clearer as we do what we know to do. The Psalmist tells us to delight in the Lord: Delight thyself also in the Lord; and he shall give thee the desires of thine heart. (Psalm 37:4). When our delight is to do His will He puts desires in our heart for particular things. When our hearts are right, our job is to pursue those desires with everything in us. Desire what God desires. And desire it for the same reason God desires it. If you do, God will give you whatever you want. God gave Joseph a dream. He held on to his dream as a slave. He held on to his dream in prison. It seemed that his dream would never come to pass but Joseph stayed busy. Whatever was done, Joseph was the doer of it. He matured and kept his heart pure before God. The Word of the Lord tried him. He was no longer that brash, cocky young man watching his father's sheep. The circumstances of life had humbled him. He saw God's hand of providence in everything he did. Praise was ordained in Joseph for a testimony. He learned to praise God and acknowledge God in everything. God exalted and blessed Joseph. He became great. Regardless of his outward condition, Joseph was great in spirit. He maintained his integrity. In every situation he honored God. In the end, Joseph's dream came to pass and God gave him the desires of his heart.

When A Baby Is Born

For many years, Christmas has been a busy time around our house. It is an exciting time for us as we anticipate our gift exchange as a family. In preparation, the girls are baking cookies and decorating. I am usually called upon to move furniture or dig something out of storage. We usually put some decorations outside as well. We are preparing to celebrate the greatest event in all of history: the Birth of Jesus.

I believe that God enjoys birthday celebrations especially the celebration of the One who saves from sin. Glad tidings to all people of the world! It is always exciting news when a baby is born. This is even true of the angels of God in heaven any time a spiritual birth occurs. Likewise, I say unto you, there is joy in the presence of the angels of God over one sinner that repenteth. (Luke 15:10). In any society a birth is news to tell. We celebrate birthdays at our home as well. All of our daughters' birthdays' fall in January, (mine is in January) February and March except for Gwen's birthday in August. As wife and mother I think she deserves her own special month don't you? In any event, the birth I am especially referring to is the birth of Jesus. In His birth, God became man and dwelt among us. Emanuel- God with us! This was good news indeed! Let's look at the events leading up to the Nativity. The Father made a big "To Do" over Jesus' birth. An angel appears to Joseph: But while he thought on these things, behold, the angel of the Lord appeared unto him in a dream, saying, Joseph, thou son of David, fear not to take unto thee Mary thy wife: for that which is conceived in her is of the Holy Ghost. (Matthew 1:20). Wise men from the east traveled a great distance because a star had appeared in the skies declaring the birth of a king. Now when Jesus was born in Bethlehem of Judaea in the days of Herod the king, behold, there came wise men from the east to Jerusalem, 2 Saying, Where is he that is born King of the Jews? for we have seen his star in the east, and are come to worship him. (Matthew 2:1-2). Gabriel appeared to Zacharias and told him that his own son's ministry (John). would prepare the way for Messiah. And he shall go before him in the spirit and power of Elias, to turn the hearts of the fathers to the children, and the disobedient to the wisdom of the just; to make ready a people prepared for the Lord. (Luke 1:17). The angel appeared to Mary and spoke to her of the birth of Jesus. And, behold, thou shalt conceive in thy womb, and bring forth a son, and shalt call his name JESUS. (Luke 1:31). Elisabeth, the wife of Zacharias and the mother of John prophesied to Mary. And she spake out with a loud voice, and said, Blessed art thou among women, and blessed is the fruit of thy womb. (Luke 1:42). God the Father sent angels to certain shepherds watching their flocks by night. And the angel said unto them, Fear not: for, behold, I bring you good tidings of great joy, which shall be to all people. 11 For unto you is born this day in the city of David a Saviour, which is Christ the Lord. (Luke 2:10-11). After this was the declaration of the just and devout man Simeon: And it was revealed unto him by the Holy Ghost, that he should not see death, before he had seen the Lord's Christ. (Luke 2:26). Then Anna, the prophetess came at that same instant: And she coming in that instant gave thanks likewise unto the Lord, and spake of him to all them that looked for redemption in Jerusalem. (Luke 2:38). What an exciting time it was and continues to be.

When We Act In Faith

When we act in faith toward God, several things take place. First of all, an act of faith pleases God. It pleases Him because we are drawing near to Him by our faith. It pleases Him because not only does our faith touch God it touches other people. When we demonstrate our faith in God we witness to the world that He is alive, He is real and we have fellowship with Him. Lastly, faith is pleasing to God because it opens an avenue for His blessings to be poured out on us. Our Heavenly Father delights in blessing His children and He wants to bless us more than we know. Our faith allows His goodness and benefits to flow toward us. When we act in faith we touch God, we touch other people and by simply trusting

Him we open the door for God's blessing to be poured out in our lives. Demonstrate your faith. An act of faith touches the heart of God and releases God's blessing to you. Abound in faith. Continue in faith so that His grace and blessing may continually be poured out.

Why Go To All The Trouble?

As I travel and preach the Word of God, I sometimes ask myself, "Why go to all the trouble?" There are more profitable ways to earn a living and still be at home with my family. We all have options in this life. God gives us a choice. Then I take the time to quiet myself before Him. I take time to come before Him and worship. I listen for His voice. He gently tells me again, "The lips of the righteous feed many." (Proverbs 10:21). And again He says to me, "Strengthen the hands of believers that they may get about the work of the ministry." (Zechariah 8:9). I hear the words that Jesus spoke, "And he said unto them, I must preach the kingdom of God to other cities also: for therefore am I sent." (Luke 4:43). He also whispers in my ear, "And this gospel of the kingdom shall be preached in all the world for a witness unto all nations; and then shall the end come." (Matthew 24:14). I so much enjoy the anointing and the presence of the Lord in our services. It comes with a price, however. I can do nothing other than obey Him and pursue the call He has given me. I love Him so much. My only ambition is to love him. Did you know He hung on a cross for me? He was beaten and bruised for me? He bled and died for me? He went to hell for me? He loves us so very much! How can I not give the best I have to Him?

Why Of Prosperity

As we live life we understand that it is God's good pleasure to bless and prosper His children. The scriptures also reveal His will to shower us with good things: For the LORD God is a sun and shield: the LORD will give grace and glory: no good thing will he withhold from them that walk uprightly. (Psalm 84:11). Who satisfieth thy mouth with good things; so that thy youth is renewed like the eagle's. (Psalm 103:5). Whoso causeth the righteous to go astray in an evil way, he shall fall himself into his own pit: but the upright shall have good things in possession. (Proverbs 28:10). If ye then, being evil, know how to give good gifts unto your children, how much more shall your Father which is in heaven give good things to them that ask him? (Matthew 7:11). He hath filled the hungry with good things; and the rich he hath sent empty away. (Luke 1:53). And how shall they preach, except they be sent? as it is written, How beautiful are the feet of them that preach the gospel of peace, and bring glad tidings of good things! (Romans 10:15). He that spared not his own Son, but delivered him up for us all, how shall he not with him also freely give us all things? (Romans 8:32). Charge them that are rich in this world, that they be not highminded, nor trust in uncertain riches, but in the living God, who giveth us richly all things to enjoy; (1 Timothy 6:17). We have understood the "WHAT" of prosperity but we have not always seen the "WHY" of prosperity. Whenever there is a "WHAT" there is also a "WHY." God gives you a car so you can use it to bring people to church. He gives you a bigger house for your comfort but also to minister to visitors. He gives you a pay raise for your family but also to bless your church and other gospel ministries. Don't forget the "WHY" of prosperity. God wants us to partner with Him in spreading the Gospel throughout the earth: But thou shalt remember the LORD thy God: for it is he that giveth thee power to get wealth, that he may establish his covenant which he sware unto thy fathers, as it is this day. (Deuteronomy 8:18). As His children, If we do not handle the "things" He gives us in a righteous manner, the "things" we desire will be withheld from us. Your iniquities have turned away these things, and your sins have withholden good things from you. (Jeremiah 5:25). Remember that it is the Lord God who supplies your need and grants your desires. When prosperity comes, our obligation is to God and His work.

A Wise Thing To Do

Only Eternity will reveal what giving to the Gospel and the work of God in the earth is accomplishing. The Bible tells us in the book of Proverbs: The fruit of the righteous is a tree of life; and he that winneth souls is wise. (Proverbs 11:30). It is wisdom to support Gospel work faithfully and consistently. To do so is to win the hearts and souls of men for Christ and it is a wise thing, it is the smart thing to do! Be encouraged! God says it is the wise thing to do!

With Help We Go

With help we are going. We are doing the work. We are preaching this glorious Gospel. Others refresh our ministry. Paul wrote letters acknowledging the help he received to preach and that is exactly what I am doing. I am grateful for the help I receive to preach this Gospel. I am glad of the coming of Stephanas and Fortunatus and Achaicus: for that which was lacking on your part they have supplied. 18 For they have refreshed my spirit and yours: therefore acknowledge ye them that are such. (1 Corinthians 16:17-18). I am ever conscious that what we do in spreading the Gospel we do it with the help of others.

A Wonderful Idea

Let us come before his presence with thanksgiving, and make a joyful noise unto him with psalms. For the LORD is a great God, and a great King above all gods. (Psalm 95:2-3). Thanksgiving is a wonderful idea! A day set apart just to give thanks! I have learned over the years to take time to count my blessings and thank God for all the good things He has bestowed upon me. We serve a great God and a wonderful Savior. We have much to be thankful for.

The Word Brings Fruit

I am taking this Gospel to hungry hearts. In upstate New York we taught the people to make room for the Holy Ghost in their Church. We were happy to see three people saved and receive Jesus for the first time in their lives and a dozen or so filled with the Holy Spirit. I am always thankful for the fruit that comes from preaching the Word of God. Through the years as we have preached, I have observed that the Word always brings forth fruit. Many times I come and I go and observe very little at the time. Sometimes, the Word we preach is not well received by a church or some of the people. In those instances we have wept and prayed and sought God wondering, what went wrong? Why was there no fruit or such negative reaction to the Word? Through the years I have discovered that no matter what appears at the time I preach, I have learned where the Word is received it brings forth fruit. Regardless of the reaction of individuals at the time, I have seen again and again fruit come forth and remain in those that receive the Word planted in their hearts. Those who do not receive the Word simply miss out on the blessing God had for them. The Gospel truly is the power of God unto salvation. God watches over His Word to bring it to pass. The Word will have its effect! It works 100% of the time. Continue to speak the Word. Continue to believe the Word because it really is the power of God unto salvation!

The Word Is Working

It is always a thrill to me when I am able to share a subject that is unfamiliar to the hearers. At first there is incredulity, the state of being unwilling or unable to believe something. Amazement and skepticism give way to wonder. Then as the Word gains a foothold in their life you can literally see the light come on. The possibility that they can live an overcoming, abundant life dawns upon them. The Word is taking root. Joy floods their soul and it is visibly seen on their countenance. The Word is working in power and glory! The message we preach is truly Good News. It will open blind eyes and set the captive free. I am not ashamed of this Gospel I preach. It is the power of God unto salvation to all who receive it and believe it. As the light comes on and understanding is gained, believers walk at a higher level than ever before. It is not just information we are offering but revelation. The Holy Spirit infuses new life and blessing into a church.

The Word Of God Will Have Its Effect!

Several years ago I was preaching to students at Penn State who had very little knowledge of salvation, God or the Bible. Throughout the afternoon, I was preaching to as few as ten or twenty students and faculty and from time to time the crowds increased to two hundred or more. Some sit and listen for a few moments, others sit or stand for thirty minutes and some listen for two or three hours throughout the afternoon. Preaching on a college campus is usually not conducive for prayer or altar calls. The Word will have its effect on hearts. The Gospel is the Power of God! Most of the time there is at least one heckler confronting me as I preach. In all their classes they are hearing little to nothing about the God of Creation, Jesus and the God of the Bible. On college campuses I have preached on Noah and the flood, Sodom and Gomorrah,

Jonah's warning to Nineveh, the creation, Adam and Eve and the fall of man. I have told them of Christ's great love, His death, burial and resurrection and the need for a changed heart, I have warned them of impending judgment and hellfire. Having been so many years in church and having read the Bible through and spending most of my time around believers, it is easy to take for granted the unbelief and ignorance many people have of God and the Bible. Our universities are fields ripe for harvest. A young man was preaching with me who, ten years before had gotten saved as a direct result of open air preaching on a college campus. He is now a pastor and has given up all for Christ. The Word of God will have its effect! Let's take every opportunity to share the Gospel of Christ while we have the ability. We have great possibilities all around us to share the Gospel. Let's take advantage of them.

The Word We Preach

The Holy Spirit spoke to my heart years ago before I began traveling that "the lips of the righteous feed many." (Proverbs 10:21). He continued whispering in my heart, "I want you to feed my people. Go and feed my people." The Word we preach is powerful and is a discerner of the thoughts and intents of the heart. Just as Hebrews 4:12 states: For the word of God is quick, and powerful, and sharper than any twoedged sword, piercing even to the dividing asunder of soul and spirit, and of the joints and marrow, and is a discerner of the thoughts and intents of the heart. The Word of God will discern our intentions and motives. The Word will cleanse our hearts and minds. Those who regularly hear God's Word will be purified and cleansed. The Word preached in power will lay open our hearts to reveal the hidden things. As we hear the Word and practice the Word we can live life with pure and righteous intentions and motives. We can hear God clearly because the lies of the enemy are exposed and we free ourselves from self-deception. Hear the Word on a daily basis. Read, listen, study and meditate the Word of God. It will produce purity of heart and cause you to be a success in all that you do. Sanctify them through thy truth: thy word is truth. (John 17:17).

Working Together

God has ordained that we function together in Christ even as our physical body functions. You are an integral part of His Body. You are indispensable to His work! God needs you! That there should be no schism in the body; but that the members should have the same care one for another. 26 And whether one member suffer, all the members suffer with it; or one member be honoured, all the members rejoice with it. 27 Now ye are the body of Christ, and members in particular. (1 Corinthians 12:25-27). We are working together so that God's will may be done on the earth. We are giving and working so that sinners might be saved, captives set free and the devil's bondage broken. What an awesome responsibility and privilege to take our place in the Body of Christ! We are heirs of God and joint heirs with Christ. We labor, sacrifice and give because we love him! We have a divine passion to complete His work in the earth! Let your light shine bright! Be a great soul winner! Become a great influence for the Gospel!

You Are God's Garden

1 Corinthians 3:9 declares, "For we are labourers together with God: ye are God's husbandry, ye are God's building." Also in Isaiah 61:3 we read, "...that they might be called trees of righteousness, the planting of the LORD, that he might be glorified." Simply put, you are God's garden. With this insight

we can understand why Jesus put such emphasis on His parable of the Sower. In Mark 4:13, "And he said unto them, Know ye not this parable? and how then will ye know all parables?" Jesus plainly states that if you do not understand this parable, all scripture concerning the Kingdom will be a mystery to you. There are three basic elements in this parable. They are the seed, external influences and the soil. The seed is the Word of God and it must be planted in our hearts. Every seed produces after its kind. The seed of the Word will produce the fruit of success, prosperity, healing, protection and salvation. We must nurture the seed of the Word and watch over it with vigilance. Without the seed there will be no fruit. The soil is your heart and there are many factors that will determine the condition of that soil. There is ground by the wayside, stony ground, thorny ground and good ground. The seed remains the same but we can work with the soil. We can fertilize the ground, cultivate the soil and, remove rocks and stones from the soil. We cultivate the soil of our hearts by being doers of the Word. By serving, giving, prayer and worship we cultivate the soil of our hearts. External influences; the devil, afflictions, persecutions, deceitfulness of riches, the cares of this life and the lust of other things are all intended to steal the seed of the Word and render it powerless in your life. We must constantly deal with these external influences and keep our hearts in a condition conducive for bringing forth fruit. One positive external influence we can pray for is the rain of the Holy Ghost. Zechariah 10:1 exhorts us to "Ask ye of the LORD rain in the time of the latter rain; so the LORD shall make bright clouds, and give them showers of rain, to every one grass in the field." The rains of God upon our heart will add moisture to the soil that is vital for a fruitful harvest.

You Are The Disciple That Jesus Loves!

The Bible tells us that Jesus was touched with the feelings of our infirmities. He knows what we know! He feels what we feel! Sometimes when we go through "fits of the flesh" and deal with just being human, it is difficult for us to relate to a God who is perfect. How do we relate with a God who has no sin and isn't right in front of us in the flesh where we can talk to Him and "vent" our feelings? I want to remind you that Jesus walked where you walk. He felt what you feel. You may think, "But I have failed and He has never failed. I hurt because of mistakes and sins and He has never sinned." Here is where we need a revelation of His love. God is love. What can that mean? Not only did Jesus walk where we walk but also His love enables Him to feel what we feel right now. Yes, He is perfect and without sin but He can feel our discouragements, our hurts, and our failings. I don't know how but He does. When I am ministering in the Holy Ghost, I can hear the prayers and feel the emotional pain of the people I am ministering to. I don't know how but I feel what they are feeling and I know what they know by the gifts of the Holy Ghost. I know God knows where we are. He loves us so! If in my insensitivity I can hurt when someone else hurts how much more does God feel and know all about us? I know He loves you and me. Pray for a greater revelation of that love. I want more of Him. I want to know His heart. I am the disciple that Jesus loves! You are the disciple that Jesus loves!

You Get What You Preach

The Word is working in Power and Glory! What a thrill and privilege it is for me to deliver the living Word of God to thirsty souls! Thank God for His Word! As we continue to preach the word on salvation, people are being saved. As we continue to preach the word on healing, people are healed. As we continue to preach the Word on the Holy Ghost, people are filled with the Spirit. I have learned through the years that you get what you preach. If healing is never preached from the pulpit no one will ever be healed. If you never preach on the Holy Ghost, you will never see anyone filled with the Spirit. Isaiah tells us, For as the rain cometh down, and the snow from heaven, and returneth not thither, but watereth the earth, and maketh it bring forth and bud, that it may give seed to the sower, and bread to the eater: So shall my word be that goeth forth out of my mouth: it shall not return unto me void, but it shall accomplish that which I please, and it shall prosper in the thing whereto I sent it. (Isaiah 55:10-11). God's Word will accomplish what it was sent forth to do.

The End

*Appendix: How To Write A Thank You Note

The following elements are included in each of my thank you letters to our ministry partners. (By no means does this cover the insights that Tim Stemple has into a thank you note.) The wisdom shared with me by Tim has been an enormous help as I continue to preach and teach the Gospel of Christ.

How To Write A Thank You Note

1. Show and acknowledge that you appreciate the gift (Thank them for the gift)

2. Show them how you are using their gift (What ministry is the gift supporting)

3. Show them that you are praying for them

4. Show them that you want them to pray for you

5. Teach them something from the Word of God (Sow Scripture back into their lives)

Never Neglect to send a thank you note- The thank you notes receive 100% readership and will be the foundation for all ministry support.

by Tim Stemple (used by permission)

Contact The Author

To order books and Cd's by Brother Gary or to contact him for speaking engagements, please email or write to:

Reach The World Ministries
Gary Bailey
PO Box 262
Hyde, PA 16843
814.290.6259

Visit our website at:

www.garybaileyministries.com

Email us at:

gbrtwm@gmail.com

www.ingramcontent.com/pod-product-compliance
Lightning Source LLC
LaVergne TN
LVHW011416080426
835512LV00005B/99